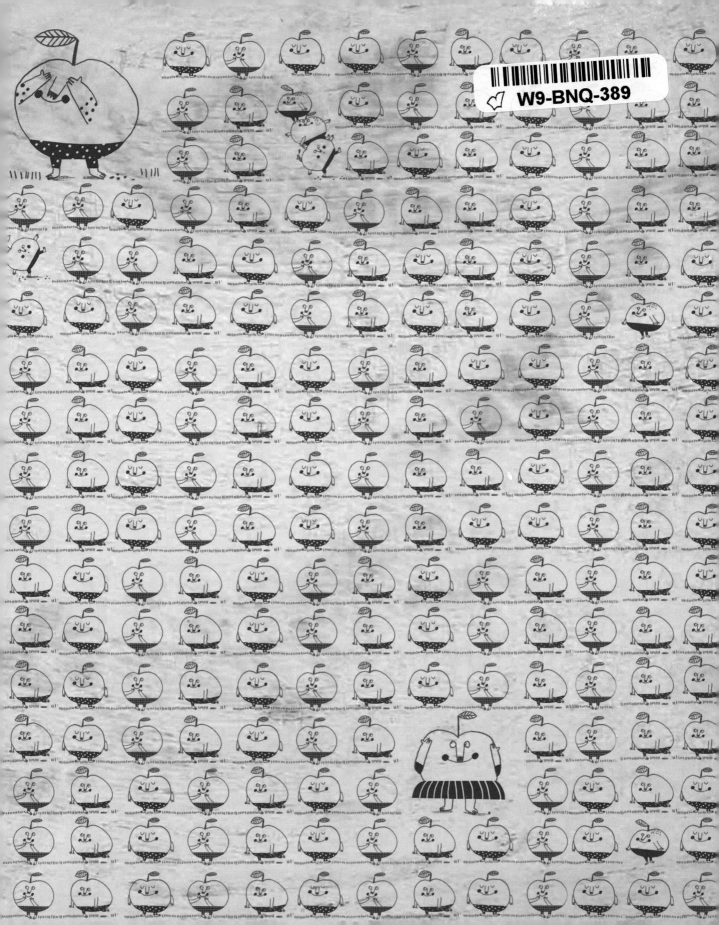

To awaken the tastebuds of my children, Arzhel and Dae, from their very first meals.

Cooking for Kids

PHOTOGRAPHY

Rina Nurra

STYLING

Lissa Streeter

ILLUSTRATIONS

Christine Roussey

ART DIRECTION

Pierre Tachon

New York · Paris · London · Milan

From Babies to Toddlers: Simple, Healthy, and Natural Food

Paule Neyrat

Alain Ducasse

Jérôme Lacressonnière

Kids

PN–The transition from bottle to spoon and the process of introducing new foods are not easy matters for new parents.

AD–And so we've written this book, to show parents how to feed infants from 6 months to 3 years, providing them with healthy, good, and natural food—all hassle-free!

PN–It's not usual for a master chef of your standing to be interested in purées, compotes, and other blended food. It's not what you serve in your starred restaurants.

AD–Of course not. But that doesn't mean I don't know how to prepare them. What I care about more than anything is that little ones gradually learn about different flavors, thanks to good ingredients rather than industrially made baby food in jars.

TERRIER

DIVERSIFICATION TABLE

	6th month	7th month	8th month	9th month	10th month
Milk	Formula				
Dairy products	Plain yogurt	+ Fromage blanc (or yogurt or unsalted ricotta)	+ Soft ripened cheese	+ Blue-veined cheese	
Organic fruit (excluding berries)	All fruit except kiwi and melon, cooked and blended (smooth). 3½ to 4½ oz. (100 to 130 g)			All fruit except kiwi and melon Raw, very ripe, and mashed 5 to 7½ oz. (150 to 200 g)	
Organic berries					
Organic vegetables	Carrot, zucchini, lettuce, Swiss chard, French beans, spinach, parsnip, pumpkin, Belgian endive, fennel, sweet potato, watercress Cooked and blended (smooth) 3½ to 4½ oz. (100 to 130 g)	+ Artichoke bottom + Garden peas Cooked and blended (smooth). 3½ to 4½ oz. (100 to 130 g)		+ Tomato + Asparagus tips + Garlic + Onion + Button mushrooms Blended with small pieces 5 to 7½ oz. (150 to 200 g)	+ Turnip + Celery + Beets Blended with small pieces 5 to 7½ oz. (150 to 200) g
Potatoes	Blended to smooth texture	Blended smooth or with vegetables			
Pulses					
Infant cereals	Gluten-free		With gluten		
Cereals		Gluten-free: corn, rice	With gluten: wheat		
Bread and other grain products			Pasta, fine couscous, rice ½ to ⅓ oz. (20 to 30 g)	Pasta, semolina, rice ⅔ oz. (20 g)	
Animal and vegetable proteins		Lean meat, poultry, fish ⅓ oz. (10 g) or 2 teaspoons Egg yolk: ¼ hard-boiled	Lean meat, poultry, fish ⅔ oz. (20 g), minced	Egg yolk: ⅓ hard-boiled	
Added fat		Olive and canola oil: 1 teaspoon Butter: 1 teaspoon (5 g) Crème fraîche: 1½ teaspoons (7.5 ml)			
Spices					
Salt	Very little	Very little	Very little	Very little	Very little
Sugar, jams	As little as possible	As little as possible	As little as possible	As little as possible	As little as possible

11th month	12th month	12 to 18 months	2nd year	3rd year
		Toddler formula	Toddler formula	
	+ Creamy desserts			
	No restrictions Raw, ripe, and mashed. 5 to 7½ oz. (150 to 200 g)	No restrictions Small pieces to chew on. 5 to 7 oz. (150 to 200 g)		
	Stewed or raw, ripe, and mashed 5 to 7½ oz. (150 to 200 g)	In small pieces to chew 5 to 7 oz. (150 to 200 g)		
	+ Cauliflower + Cabbage Blended with small pieces. 5 to 7 oz. (150 to 200 g)	+ Eggplant + Bell pepper Blended with small pieces. 5 to 7 oz. (150 to 200 g)	All, depending on the infant's appetite, raw and cooked	
			Mashed smooth	
		Blended starting from 18 months		
	+ Bread, depending on Baby's appetite			
	Shellfish and crustaceans, if no allergy risk	Lean meat, poultry, fish 1 oz. (30 g) chopped or small pieces Shellfish and crustaceans at 18 months if risk of allergy Egg: ½	Lean meat, poultry, fish 1½ oz. (40 g) minced or in small pieces Tofu Whole egg: 1	Lean meat, poultry, fish 2 oz. (50 g) chopped or small pieces
	1 small pinch			
Very little	Very little	Very little	Very little	Very little
As little as possible	As little as possible	As little as possible	As little as possible	As little as possible

Vegetable Garden

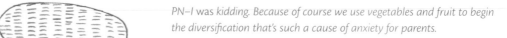

PN–What a lot of recipes in this small vegetable garden: Purées, soups, potatoes, small dishes of fresh vegetables. We all know how much you love vegetables—is that why?

AD–Are you kidding? Yes, I adore vegetables but you of all people don't need any lessons on how important they are in our diet.

PN–I was kidding. Because of course we use vegetables and fruit to begin the diversification that's such a cause of anxiety for parents.

AD–With this choice of recipes that start for six-month-olds, they should be completely reassured. And we'll gradually educate Baby's palate, starting with her very first purées.

PN–Yes, we introduce the various vegetables according to how strong their flavors are and how easily they are digested, working up to the age of two, when babies can eat them all without any problem.

AD–But only ORGANIC VEGETABLES! They're best for educating little ones' palates and for their health, as well as from every other point of view.

PN–We don't repeat this advice on every page; it goes without saying. I see you've also concocted some delicious recipes with pulses.

AD–They're suitable for the whole family. Just use a fork to mash what you need for your little one.

PN–And that's SIMPLER, HEALTHIER, and BETTER! You've learned the lesson, Chef.

Purée

Carrot and Pumpkin

AD–When fresh bunched carrots aren't in season, use small carrots that don't have a tough core. And of course they must be nice and fresh, and firm, not flaccid! You can easily replace the pumpkin with Hokkaido or butternut squash.

PN–Best wait until your infant is one year old to introduce her to turmeric and ginger—they both make the mouth tingle. If you don't have the fresh rhizomes, just use a tiny pinch of ground turmeric or ginger.

Carrot purée

… Wash and peel 7 ounces (200 g) of fresh bunched carrots, about 4 carrots, and slice them finely.

… Steam them for 15 minutes.

… Blend them, gradually adding a little formula, until the purée is smooth.

Pumpkin purée

… Carefully remove the stringy fibers and seeds from 7 ounces (200 g) of pumpkin flesh. Cut it into small cubes.

… Steam the cubes, then blend them, gradually adding a little formula, just as you did for the carrots.

Carrot and orange purée

… Wash 1 unwaxed orange. Squeeze half for the juice and strain it into a cup.

… Blend the cooked carrots with the orange juice and a little formula. Add 2 to 3 pinches of finely grated orange zest into the purée.

Carrot and cilantro purée

… Wash 3 leaves of cilantro (coriander). Add together with the formula when you make the Carrot Purée.

LATER, ABOUT 12 MONTHS

Carrot purée with turmeric

… Wash and peel a small piece of fresh turmeric. Cut a piece weighing ⅓ ounce (10 g) and add it to the carrots when you cook them. When done, blend with some formula.

Pumpkin purée with ginger

… Wash and peel a small piece of fresh ginger. Add 2 finely grated pinches to the pumpkin cubes. Steam and process with some formula.

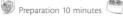

Purée

Zucchini, Swiss Chard, Lettuce, and Parsley

AD–Once Baby is used to these vegetables, have him taste the leaves of a small sprig of thyme or savory (fresh, not dried) while you're doing your cooking. Try basil, parsley, and chervil too.

PN–Turn these purées into mousses: Blend the vegetables and then whip them up with a spoonful or two of plain yogurt. Or make them into soups by increasing the amount of milk.

Zucchini and potato purée

… Carefully wash 1 medium zucchini weighing about 5 ounces (150 g). Remove the tips and cut into cubes, leaving the skin.

… Peel and wash 1 small potato weighing about 2 ounces (50 g) and cut into cubes the same size as the zucchini.

… Steam the vegetables for 15 minutes. Blend, gradually adding some formula, until you have a smooth purée.

Swiss chard and potato purée

… Wash 1 leaf of Swiss chard. Separate the green part from the rib and shred it coarsely. Peel the rib to remove long fibers and cut it into small pieces.

… Steam the green part and cut-up rib together for 15 minutes.

… Peel, wash, and dice 1 medium potato weighing about 3½ ounces (100 g).

… Steam the Swiss chard leaf and potato for 15 minutes. Blend, gradually adding some formula.

Lettuce and potato purée

… Wash 3½ ounces (100 g) of seasonal lettuce leaves (butter lettuce, escarole, oak leaf, romaine, or mâche, also known as lamb's lettuce). Remove any ribs that seem too hard and cut the leaves into a chiffonade.

… Wash, peel, and dice 1 medium potato weighing about 3½ ounces (100 g).

… Steam the vegetables for about 15 minutes. Blend, gradually adding a little formula.

Lettuce (or zucchini or Swiss chard), parsley, and potato purée

… Wash 5 to 6 sprigs of flat-leaf parsley or chervil. Pick off the leaves, chop them, and add them to the blended purée.

Purée

Belgian Endive, Spinach, and Fennel

Belgian endive, potato, and chervil purée

... Wash 1 white Belgian endive and carefully remove the hard core at the base. Cut it in half lengthwise and finely slice one half. (Keep the other half for a soup or dish for the rest of the family.)

... Wash and peel 1 medium potato weighing about 3½ ounces (100 g) and cut it into small pieces.

... Steam all the vegetables together for 15 minutes.

... Rinse and pat dry 1 branch of chervil. Pick off the leaves and chop them.

... Blend all the ingredients, adding a little formula, until the purée is smooth.

Spinach, potato, and parsley purée

... Wash 2 ounces (50 g) of fresh spinach leaves and pick off the stems. Peel 1 large potato weighing 5 ounces (150 g).

... Steam the vegetables together for 15 minutes.

... Rinse and pat dry 1 branch of flat-leaf parsley. Pick off the leaves and chop them.

... Blend all the ingredients, adding a little formula, until the purée is smooth.

Fennel and potato purée

... Wash one quarter of a fennel bulb and cut it into small pieces.

... Wash and peel 1 large potato weighing about 5 ounces (150 g) and cut it into small pieces.

... Steam the vegetables together for 15 minutes.

... Blend them together, gradually adding some formula and a little of the cooking liquid until the purée is smooth.

Fennel and apple purée

... Replace the potato with 5 ounces (150 g) of apple, preferably a Golden Delicious or other cooking apple (we use *reinettes*; ask at the greenmarket for the best local heirloom varieties), peeled and diced.

AD–These vegetables have a fairly strong flavor, which is made less intense by the potatoes. You can also replace the potatoes with sweet potatoes, using the same quantities. PN–Once your baby is over 7 months old, you can grate about 1 heaping tablespoon (⅓ ounce or 10 g) of a tasty hard cheese, such as Emmental, into the purées.

Leek, Celeriac, and Turnip

AD–When Baby is used to the taste of celeriac, finely chop a few small leaves from a celery stalk and add them to the purée at the last minute. Heirloom golden ball turnips are a wonderful vegetable to introduce to Baby if you can find any.

PN–Celeriac and turnip are not easily digested, so wait patiently until Baby is 10 months old. All these vegetables are high in fiber so blend them well! In summer, replace the leeks with green beans. Be sure to remove the strings carefully.

Leek, potato, and chive purée

… Wash and peel 1 large potato weighing about 5 ounces (150 g) and cut into small pieces. Slice 2 ounces (50 g) of leek white.

… Steam for 15 minutes.

… Wash, dry, and snip 2 sprigs of chives.

… Blend the two vegetables with the chives, gradually adding a little formula, until the purée is smooth.

STARTING FROM 10 MONTHS

Celeriac, potato, and chervil purée

… Wash and peel 3½ ounces (100 g) of celeriac and 1 medium potato weighing 3½ ounces (100 g). Cut the vegetables into small pieces.

… Steam the vegetables for 25 minutes.

… Rinse 1 sprig of chervil. Pick off the leaves and chop them.

… Blend the vegetables and chervil, gradually adding a little formula, until the purée is smooth.

Turnip, potato, and parsley purée

… Wash and peel 3½ ounces (100 g) of turnip and 3½ ounces (100 g) of potato. Cut into small pieces.

… Rinse 1 sprig of flat-leaf parsley. Pick off the leaves and chop them.

… Blend the vegetables and chervil, gradually adding a little formula, until the purée is smooth.

Celeriac (or turnip) and apple purée

… Instead of the potato, use 3½ ounces (100 g) of an apple, preferably Golden Delicious or other cooking apple (we use *reinettes*; ask at the greenmarket for the best local heirloom varieties).

Purée

Artichoke and Garden Peas

AD–Try fava beans instead of peas if you see them at the market – the season is very short. Tarragon also goes well with peas. And give Baby one or two basil leaves in the artichoke purée once he's used to the taste of the vegetable.

PN–To get Baby used to pieces (around 8 to 9 months) set aside a few of the smallest peas before you blend the mixture, and let him eat them as a finger food.

Artichoke and potato purée

… Cut off the stalk of 1 artichoke. Detach all the leaves until the heart is exposed and trim it so that the top is straight. Remove the choke (the small hairs) with a teaspoon and dice the bottom. You should be left with about 5 ounces (150 g). Place the dice in a small bowl of water and add the juice of half a lemon.

… Peel and wash 1 medium potato weighing about 3½ ounces (100 g) and cut it into pieces the same size as the artichoke bottom.

… Steam the vegetables for 15 minutes.

… Blend, gradually adding a little formula and 1 teaspoon of olive oil until the purée is smooth.

Pea purée

… Shell 7 ounces (200 g) of fresh garden peas. Peel one quarter of a medium white onion and slice it.

… Steam the vegetables with 1 sprig of savory until tender.

… Remove the savory and blend the peas and potatoes, gradually adding a little formula, until the purée is smooth.

… Stir in 1 teaspoon (5 g) of salted butter.

Pea purée with mint

… Wash 1 or 2 leaves of fresh mint and chop them. Add to the purée when you blend it.

Pea purée with fresh sheep's or cow's milk cheese

… Arrange the purée in a plate and top with 1½ teaspoons of fresh sheep or cow's milk cheese.

Main Dish

Green Asparagus and Eggs Mimosa

Prepare the vegetables
… Wash 3 or 4 green asparagus spears. Cut off the base of the tip, which is too hard to eat, and peel the spears. Cut off the tips so that they are just under 1 inch (2 cm) long. Finely slice the spears.
… Wash half a scallion, remove the outer skin, and slice it.
… Wash 2 large spinach leaves, remove the stalks, and chop the leaves roughly.
… Steam all the vegetables for 10 minutes.

Prepare the egg
… While the vegetables are steaming, place 1 egg in boiling water for 10 minutes to hard-boil. Cool it under cold running water and remove the shell.

Prepare the creamy soup
… Place the asparagus tips in a small plate and cut them into very small pieces, or mash them with a fork.
… Blend the remaining vegetables with 1 teaspoon of crème fraîche (or heavy cream) and ⅔ cup (150 ml) of formula.

To finish
… Scoop out the egg yolk and cut off one-third, keeping the rest for another use. Mash it into coarse crumbs with a fork.
… Pour the creamy soup into a bowl, add the small pieces of asparagus tips, and scatter with the egg yolk. Drizzle with a few drops of whipping cream.

AD–Of course, white asparagus, if available, also works for this recipe. But a nice velvety green with the yellow of the egg yolk is more attractive. And getting food to look nice is part of educating a child's taste. PN–You might want to add just a tiny pinch of salt, but the combination of asparagus and spinach is strong enough not to need salting. The number of asparagus spears you need depends on how big they are.

 Preparation 15 minutes Cooking 10 minutes

Angel Hair Pasta with Mushrooms

AD—Here's a good way to introduce Baby to mushrooms. Later, when she's over one year old, make this soup with star-shaped pasta and fresh chanterelles.

PN—Just a pinch of salt in the pasta is enough, so you won't need to add any to the mushrooms. Blend them if Baby is still reluctant to eat pieces. You can find both gluten-free and organic rice angel hair pasta.

.

Prepare the mushrooms

… Clean 2 ounces (50 g) of button mushrooms, removing the stem entirely. Dry well and cut into very small pieces. You should be left with about 1 ounce (30 g).

… Heat 1 teaspoon of olive oil in a small pan. Place the mushroom pieces in the pan and sauté them for 3 to 4 minutes over medium heat until they are cooked through and very tender.

Prepare the angel hair pasta

… Heat ¾ cup (200 ml) of formula and season it lightly with salt.

… When it comes to a boil, drop in ⅔ ounce (20 g) of angel hair pasta and cook for the length of time indicated on the package.

… Drain the pasta well. Mash with a fork and return to the saucepan.

To finish

… Add the mushrooms to the saucepan.

… Mix well and serve.

9 months

Purée

Pistou

… Bring some water to a boil in a saucepan. Prepare a bowl filled with cold water and ice cubes to refresh the herbs.

… Rinse 10 sprigs of basil and pick off the leaves. Dip them in the boiling water for 2 minutes, then remove them with a slotted spoon and transfer immediately to the ice water.

… Drain well and blend with 1 tablespoon plus 1 teaspoon (20 ml) of olive oil.

… Add 2 teaspoons (10 ml) of grated Parmesan and blend again.

… Squeeze the juice of one quarter of a lemon and add it to the pistou. Blend again until perfectly smooth.

… Store in an airtight container and chill.

Basil and arugula pistou

… Wash 1 handful of arugula leaves and dry well.

… Prepare the pistou as above, adding 10 sprigs of basil, leaves picked, to the arugula leaves.

Herb pistou

… Follow the same method, using 10 sprigs of parsley, 10 sprigs of chervil, and 10 sprigs of chives.

AD—These pistou recipes will be useful for dressing up a purée once Baby is used to the flavors of each of the vegetables. They'll also be delicious later, with small pasta.

PN—I like these pistous because they're full of vitamins. The herb pistou is especially useful in the winter, when you have to make do with seasonal fruit and vegetables that aren't exactly bursting with vitamins, especially not with vitamin C.

Zucchini, Scallion, and Veal

AD–When it's not zucchini season (and there is a season even if you can find them year-round), carrots or leeks go very well with veal. So does a mixture of carrots and turnips.

PN–Season the zucchini and onion purée with 1 teaspoon of grated Parmesan. This means there's no need to add the pinch of salt. And of course ⅔ ounce (20 g) of nice tender beef is just as good as veal.

Prepare the zucchini and onion

… Wash 1 medium zucchini weighing about 5 ounces (150 g). Cut off the tips and dice it finely.

… Remove the outer skin of 1 small scallion, keeping about 2 to 2½ inches (5 to 6 cm) of the stalk. Remove the top of the green part, which is hard, and snip the rest.

… Steam the vegetables with 1 sprig of savory for 6 minutes.

Prepare the veal

… Use a brush to lightly oil a small pan. Heat it gently and place ⅔ ounce (20 g) of a veal cutlet in it. Turn the heat up to high and cook the meat for 2 to 3 minutes until it is very lightly browned and soft all through.

… Mince the meat and set it aside on a small plate, keeping it warm.

To finish

… Rinse and dry 1 or 2 sprigs of flat-leaf parsley. Pick off the leaves. Chop 3 or 4 leaves and incorporate them into the chopped veal.

… Set aside 1 tablespoon of cooked zucchini and scallion.

… Blend the remaining vegetables with the savory, the parsley leaves, 1 teaspoon of olive oil, and 1 very small pinch of salt.

… Place this purée in a plate. Stir in the finely diced vegetables. Make a little hollow on the top and spoon in the minced veal.

Soup

Ways with Beets

Beet soup

… Peel and rinse 5 ounces (150 g) of a cooked beet.

… Cut off a piece and dice it finely—you'll want the equivalent of 1½ teaspoons. Place the diced beets in a bowl.

… Cut the remaining beet into larger pieces and blend with ⅔ cup (150 ml) of formula until the soup is smooth.

… Pour half of it into a bowl. Cover with plastic wrap and chill.

… Freeze the other half.

Beet soup, fromage blanc, and chives

… Rinse and finely chop 1 chive sprig. Mix three-quarters of the chopped chives with 2 teaspoons of partially skimmed fromage blanc (20 percent butterfat), unsalted ricotta, or plain yogurt.

… Dip a spoon into some hot water and shape a scoop of the fromage blanc (or alternative ingredient). Place it carefully on the top of the bowl of soup and sprinkle with the remaining chopped chives.

Beet soup and black Muscat grapes

… Wash 10 black Muscat grapes. With the tip of a small, sharp knife, remove the skin and seeds. Cut 5 grapes into small pieces, enough to fill about 2 teaspoons. Set aside.

… Blend the remaining grapes with some of the beet soup.

… Pour into a bowl and sprinkle with the small pieces of grapes.

AD–When using raw beets, wash them before cooking, but don't peel them. Either boil them for 1 hour in salted water, or steam them, or wrap them in foil and bake at 350°F (180°C) for at least 1 hour, until tender. PN–Beets contain a red pigment called betacyanin. It protects the heart but because it's water-soluble, it may color urine or stool. So don't worry if Baby's diapers are reddish— there's no danger whatsoever.

Soup

AD–Melons, apricots, or cucumbers could all be used instead of the watermelon. Play with the colors of the tomatoes, depending on what you find at the market. Just make sure they're ripe!

PN–Of course you mustn't use raw, green tomatoes, which contain solanine, a toxic substance that adults can tolerate, but not babies. If you like, add just a pinch of salt to this gazpacho, or a little canola oil, rich in omega-3, instead of the olive oil.

Ways with Tomatoes

Tomato gazpacho

… Wash 2 vine ripe tomatoes and 1 ripe yellow tomato. Remove the base and peel them. Cut into pieces, carefully removing all the seeds.

… Cut half the yellow tomato into small dice. Set aside in a cup.

… Rinse 4 leaves of basil and chop them roughly.

… Cut ⅔ ounce (20 g) of bread into small dice.

… Blend the remaining tomatoes together with the basil, the bread, and 1 teaspoon of olive oil. The gazpacho should be smooth.

… Add a few drops of lemon juice and 3 tablespoons (40 ml) of mineral water.

… Pour half the gazpacho into a bowl and spoon the yellow tomato dice over the top.

… Freeze the other half of the gazpacho.

FROM 12 MONTHS
Tomato and watermelon gazpacho

… Prepare the gazpacho in the same way, replacing the yellow tomato with 5 ounces (150 g) of watermelon. Carefully remove all the watermelon seeds. Before you blend the ingredients, set aside a small piece of watermelon. Blend the tomato and watermelon.

… Finely dice the remaining watermelon and place the dice in the bowl with the tomato gazpacho.

Soup

Zucchini, Scallion, and Herbs

Prepare the soup

… Wash 1 medium zucchini weighing about 5 ounces (150 g). Remove the tips and cut it in half lengthwise. With a teaspoon, remove the seeds. Finely dice the flesh.

… Peel and wash one half of a scallion and slice it.

… Steam the zucchini pieces and scallion for 10 minutes.

… Set aside about 2 teaspoons of diced zucchini.

… Rinse 2 mint leaves, 2 parsley leaves, and 2 cilantro leaves and chop them roughly.

… Blend the remaining zucchini, onions, herbs, and 2 teaspoons of fromage blanc (or unsalted ricotta or plain yogurt) until the soup is smooth.

… Squeeze the juice of one quarter of a lime.

… Add 3 tablespoons (40 ml) of mineral water, 1 teaspoon of olive oil, and the lime juice. Blend again to combine well.

To finish

… Let the soup cool and chill it for 15 to 20 minutes. Don't let it become icy!

… Pour it into a bowl. Add the diced zucchini and 1 teaspoon of fromage blanc (or alternative ingredient).

AD—Here's a recipe you can make for the rest of the family, or when you have friends over for a summer dinner.
PN—If you find small zucchini that are blooming, blend them without cooking them. But wait until Baby is 11 or 12 months old and already accustomed to eating pieces, because they will be raw and this soup should have some small pieces.

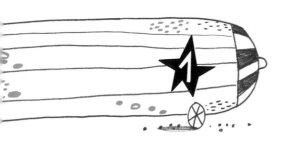

10 months

AD–Set aside one or two leaves of each of the herbs every time you prepare this creamy soup. Have Baby taste them to introduce her to their flavors.

PN–Wow! This soup really concentrates those vitamins and minerals. Baby will be bursting with energy. And parents can make some for themselves. The lettuce can also be replaced with lamb's lettuce.

Herbs and Lettuce

Prepare the potato

… Peel and wash 1 medium potato weighing about 5 ounces (150 g). Cut it into small pieces and steam for 10 minutes.

Prepare the herbs and lettuce

… Rinse 10 sprigs of chervil, 10 sprigs of flat-leaf parsley, and 5 sprigs of watercress. Pick off all the leaves.

… Take 5 large leaves of a lettuce. Wash them and remove the ribs. Chop them roughly.

… Rinse 3 leaves of mint and set aside.

… Bring some lightly salted water to a boil in a saucepan. Prepare a bowl filled with water and ice cubes.

… Drop all the herbs (with the exception of the mint), watercress, and lettuce into the boiling water. Cook for 2 minutes, remove with a slotted spoon, and immediately drop into the ice water.

… Drain well. Gather them together with your hands and squeeze well to remove as much water as possible.

Prepare the creamy soup

… Heat ¾ cup (200 ml) of formula.

… Blend the potato, herbs, and lettuce, gradually adding the hot milk.

… Stir in 1 teaspoon of heavy cream.

… Finely chop the mint leaves and add.

… Blend again until the soup is very smooth. Test the temperature and pour it into a bowl or bottle.

Main Dish

Potato, Asparagus, and Quail Egg

AD–If you find wild green asparagus at the market, grab it! It has a marvelously delicate taste and, even better, you won't have to peel it. But you'll need about four spears because they are very thin.

PN–Quail's eggs are practical: they save you cutting one-third from a hard-boiled hen's egg – that's the ration up to 10 months. No need to add salt to the purée because this recipe calls for salted butter.

Prepare the potato and asparagus

… Peel 1 large potato weighing 5 ounces (150 g). Cut into small pieces and place in the steaming basket.

… Trim off the tips of 2 green asparagus, about 1¼ inches (3 cm). Wash them and remove the bracts. Place them in the steaming basket with the pieces of potato.

… Steam for 5 to 7 minutes and remove the asparagus.

… Cook the potatoes for another 10 minutes, until tender.

Prepare the quail egg

… Bring some water to a boil in a saucepan. Place 1 quail egg in it and cook until hard, about 4 minutes.

… Cool under cold running water and peel. Remove the yolk and mash it with a fork. Set aside on a small plate.

Prepare the purée

… With a masher, mash the potato. Add 1 teaspoon (5 g) of salted butter and thin the purée with a little formula. Don't add any salt.

To finish

… Spoon the mashed potato onto a plate. Make a little hollow in the center and place the mashed egg yolk in it.

… Cut the asparagus tips in half lengthwise and stand them in the mashed potato, around the egg yolk.

Soup

12 months

Ways with Pumpkin

Pumpkin and chestnut soup

… Prepare (or defrost) 1 serving of pumpkin purée (p. 10).

… Place it in a saucepan and gradually add formula until it is liquid but not too thin.

… Wash, peel, and snip half a small scallion.

… With a brush, grease a small nonstick pan with 1 drop of olive oil and 1 small knob of butter, just under 1 teaspoon (3 to 4 g).

<u>Heat the pan and gently soften the onion, taking care that it does not color.</u>

… Add 3 to 4 chestnuts (either vacuum-packed or jarred) and 1 sprig of thyme. Cook gently for 10 minutes, stirring frequently.

… Remove the thyme. Mash the chestnuts lightly with a fork and add them to the pumpkin soup.

Pumpkin, Roquefort, and hazelnut soup

… Heat 1 serving of pumpkin purée (p. 10) and thin it with some formula.

… Cut ⅓ ounce (10 g) of Roquefort (or other blue cheese) into small pieces.

… Pour the soup into a bowl and sprinkle with the Roquefort and 1 teaspoon of ground hazelnuts (or almonds).

Pumpkin, grapes, and goat's milk cheese

… Wash 5 green grapes. Peel them and cut them in halves. With the tip of a knife, remove all the seeds. Cut the grapes into small pieces.

… Heat 1 serving of pumpkin purée (p. 10) and thin it with some formula.

… Cut ⅓ ounce (10 g) of soft, fresh goat's milk cheese into small pieces.

… Pour the soup into a bowl and sprinkle with goat's milk cheese and grape pieces.

AD–This pumpkin-hazelnut soup is nice and mild! In fact, its mildness counters the strong taste of Roquefort. Try it with other veined cheeses so Baby can get to know the whole range. No grapes? Use some finely diced Granny Smith apple.
PN–You should definitely not add salt to soups that have cheese—there's enough in the cheese already! If there are any allergies to nuts in the family, wait for Baby to turn 3 before you serve him this pumpkin-hazelnut soup.

Purée

Broccoli and Cauliflower

AD–These two vegetables are interchangeable. Buy whichever one you find at the market, depending on the season. Sweet potato or pear will sweeten their taste, which is pretty strong. When Baby is a little older, use either broccoli or cauliflower alone, with the parsley and tofu.

PN–There's no need for meat, fish, or poultry the day you serve the broccoli and tofu purée. That's because tofu has as much protein as animal protein. But a little grated cheese will be good with the other purées.

Broccoli and sweet potato purée

… Wash about 3½ ounces (100 g) of broccoli florets. Remove any stems that seem too hard.

… Peel a piece of sweet potato (or 1 potato) weighing about 3½ ounces (100 g) and cut it into small pieces.

… First steam the sweet potato for 5 to 7 minutes. Add the broccoli florets and continue for a further 10 minutes. Blend, adding formula and 1 teaspoon of olive oil, until you have a smooth purée.

Broccoli purée with parsley

… Prepare the broccoli and potato purée as above, setting aside 2 to 3 uncooked broccoli florets.

… Wash and chop 10 leaves of flat-leaf parsley. Grate the uncooked broccoli florets.

… Add the grated broccoli to the purée with the chopped parsley.

Broccoli and tofu purée

… Cut ⅔ ounce (20 g) of tofu into very small dice. Stir it into one of these purées.

Cauliflower and pear purée

… Wash 5 ounces (150 g) of cauliflower florets and steam for 15 minutes. Blend with 1 teaspoon (5 g) of butter and gradually add a little formula until the purée is perfectly smooth.

… Peel half of a juicy pear and cut it into quarters. Remove the seeds and core and cut it into very small pieces. Stir them into the purée.

 Purée

Cauliflower and Apple

AD—Cooked and raw, tender and crunchy—a great combination to awaken little taste buds. You can add a touch of grated Parmesan, just mix it in with the grated florets. You can also make this recipe with broccoli. PN—I really like dishes with raw ingredients! It means there are more vitamins and it's good for Baby to get used to eating food that's not so soft. This dish can be made for the whole family: Just mash what you need for the little one.

Prepare the cauliflower and the apple

… Rinse 3½ to 4 ounces (100 to 120 g) of cauliflower florets. Set aside 2 or 3.

… Peel half of a Granny Smith apple. Remove the core and cut it in 2. Set aside one quarter. Cut the other into small pieces.

… Steam the florets and apple pieces for 10 to 12 minutes, until tender.

… Set aside 4 florets in a small plate and keep warm.

… With a fork, mash the rest with the apple pieces. Keep this purée warm.

To finish

… Finely dice the apple quarter and place the pieces in a small bowl.

… Grate the reserved 2 or 3 raw cauliflower florets and drizzle with a few drops of lemon juice.

… Stir 1 teaspoon of olive oil into the cauliflower-apple purée, and then add the reserved cooked florets. Combine well and transfer to the plate.

… Top the purée with the mixture of raw grated cauliflower and diced apple and serve.

Main Dish

French Beans, Tomato, and Garlic

Prepare the French beans

… Wash and trim 2 ounces (50 g) of extra-fine French beans. Cut them into small pieces.

… Peel and wash 1 small scallion, keeping 1¼ inches (3 cm) of the stalk. Cut it into pieces the same size as the beans.

… Steam the vegetables together for 8 to 10 minutes, until tender, then blend them lightly, making sure to leave the texture a little lumpy.

Prepare the tomato

… While the vegetables are steaming, wash and peel 1 medium red tomato weighing about 3½ ounces (100 g) and remove the seeds. Dice it.

… Peel 1 garlic clove, cut it in two, and remove the shoot. Chop one-third of the clove.

… Heat 1 teaspoon of olive oil in a small pan over low heat and cook the chopped garlic. Add the chopped tomato and cook for 5 to 7 minutes, keeping the heat low, until it is very soft.

To finish

… Rinse, dry, and chop 2 or 3 leaves of flat-leaf parsley.

… Heat a small nonstick pan and toast 1 teaspoon of sesame seeds until they are lightly colored. Drain them on a paper towel.

… Place the blended green beans and onion in the pan with the tomatoes. Season very lightly with salt and mix.

… Sprinkle with chopped parsley and sesame seeds and serve.

AD—Usually, extra-fine French beans don't have any strings. If they are a little thicker, remove them carefully. When you toast the sesame seeds, prepare a larger amount to use for the rest of the family.

PN—Decide on the quantity of beans according to your baby's appetite. If you make this for the main meal, you can add 1 ounce (30 g) of cooked cold chicken breast, chopped, for a wholesome dish.

Purée

Summer Vegetables

… Wash 1 medium zucchini weighing 4 to 5 ounces (120 to 150 g). Don't peel it, just remove the tips. Cut it into small dice.

… Wash 1 small tomato weighing 2 to 2½ ounces (50 to 70 g). Remove the base and dip it into boiling water for 10 seconds. Cool it under cold running water and remove the skin. Discard all the seeds and cut it into pieces.

… From 1 eggplant, cut a piece weighing 2 to 2½ ounces (50 to 70 g). Half-peel it with a vegetable peeler, leaving alternate strips of skin down the length. Remove all the seeds. Cut it into small pieces.

… Steam the vegetables with 1 sprig of lemon thyme and half a bay leaf for 15 minutes.

… Rinse 2 basil leaves and chop them coarsely.

… Discard the thyme and bay leaf. Blend the vegetables with 1 teaspoon of olive oil, the basil, and 1 small pinch of salt.

AD–It's best to wait until Baby is 12 months old to introduce eggplant. Mixed with zucchini and tomato, it should go over well. Later, change the proportions to increase the quantity of eggplant. Baby should have no problem getting used to this vegetable. PN–If you remove some of the skin, the taste of the eggplant is not so strong. You can simply mash these vegetables—by this stage, Baby is used to small pieces.

Melon and Mango

AD–Start off with a plain soup, either melon or mango, to introduce Baby to the taste of each fruit. When she's used to both, move on to these recipes, and let her suck on a leaf of fresh mint.

PN–These two recipes are perfectly suitable for the entire family. Just adapt the quantities depending on your little one's appetite. Melon, mango, and raspberry are all full of antioxidants. Little ones need them as much as grown-ups!

Melon and raspberry soup

… Cut 1 small ripe cantaloupe into 4 pieces. Set aside 3 pieces for the rest of the family. With a teaspoon, remove all the seeds and any fibers from the piece for Baby.

… Cut out all the flesh and blend it with 3 tablespoons (50 ml) of low-mineral bottled water, leaving the texture a little lumpy.

… Pour it into a bowl and chill.

… Pick out 10 ripe raspberries. With a fork, crush 7 of them in a plate.

… Add them to the soup with the 3 remaining whole raspberries and serve.

Mint-flavored mango soup

… Peel 1 ripe mango and cut off the flesh. Take one quarter for Baby and set aside the rest for the other members of the family.

… Cut the equivalent of 2 teaspoons into small dice and place them in a cup.

… Rinse 1 small sprig of fresh mint. Roughly chop 2 leaves.

… Blend the rest of the quarter mango with the chopped mint and a little mineral water if necessary.

… Pour the soup into a bowl, add the diced mango, and garnish with the small sprig of mint.

Main Dish

Sweet Potato, Bacon, and Red Onion

Prepare the sweet potato and onion

… Peel and wash 5 ounces (150 g) of a sweet potato and one quarter of a red onion (about ⅔ ounce or 20 g).

… Finely dice the sweet potato and cut the onion into fine slices.

… Steam together for 10 to 15 minutes, until both vegetables are very tender.

… Mash them with a fork and keep warm.

Prepare the bacon

… Remove as much fat as possible from a piece of bacon; you should be left with about ⅔ ounce (20 g). Heat a small pan over high heat and cook it on both sides until it is slightly crisp. When it is done, pat it with paper towel to absorb any excess fat.

… Cut it into small dice.

To finish

… Turn on broiler.

… Transfer the mashed sweet potato and onion mixture to a small heatproof dish or pan.

… Mix in the diced bacon.

… Remove the rind from a ⅓-ounce (10 g) slice of Reblochon or raclette cheese and set it over the dish.

… Place in the oven and broil until the cheese has melted.

… Let cool a little before serving.

AD–An introduction to sweet-savory combinations! When you cook the bacon, make sure it remains fairly soft so that Baby can eat it easily. If the pieces are too dry, she might complain and spit them out. PN–Important: no salt in the sweet potato. There's more than enough in the bacon and the cheese. A thin slice of Emmental cheese is also fine for this take on a dish from the Alps called tartiflette.

Potato, Olives, and Sea Bream

AD–If this is the first time your little one will be eating olives, have her taste them first with the mashed potato before you give her a small piece of an olive on its own.
PN–No need to add salt to the mashed potatoes—the olives take care of that. Adapt the quantity of olives to your baby's appetite.

Prepare the potato and sea bream

… Wash and peel 2 potatoes weighing about 5 ounces (150 g) altogether. Cut them into small pieces.
… Check that there are no bones in 1 sea bream fillet weighing 1 ounce (30 g).
… Steam the potatoes with 1 sprig of thyme and half a bay leaf for 10 minutes.
… Place the fish fillet over the potato pieces and steam for a further 5 minutes.

Prepare the olives

… While the potatoes are cooking, pit 3 small black olives.
… Cut the flesh into very small dice.

To finish

… With a fork, mash the potatoes, adding 1 teaspoon of olive oil.
… Mix in the diced olives.
… Place the mashed potatoes with olives in a plate and make a little hollow in the top.
… Flake the sea bream fillet and place the pieces in the hollow. Drizzle with a few drops of lemon juice and serve.

Main Dish

Ratatouille

Prepare the vegetables

… Wash 1 small zucchini weighing about 3½ ounces (100 g). Trim the ends and dice it finely.

… Remove the outer skin of 1 small scallion and chop it finely.

… Peel 1 medium tomato weighing about 3½ ounces (100 g). Remove the seeds and dice it.

… Take 1 eggplant and cut a piece weighing about 3½ ounces (100 g). Half-peel it with a vegetable peeler, leaving alternate strips of skin. Carefully remove all the seeds and cut the flesh into small dice.

Cook the ratatouille

… Rinse 1 clove of garlic, leaving the skin on. Prick it with the tip of a knife.

… In a small sauté pan, heat 2 teaspoons of olive oil. Sauté the chopped scallion for 2 to 3 minutes, ensuring that it does not color.

… Add all the vegetables, the garlic, 1 small sprig of thyme, 1 very small piece of bay leaf, and 1 small pinch of salt.

… Combine the ingredients and cook over high heat for 2 to 3 minutes, then lower the heat and cook for about 10 minutes, until the vegetables are well softened.

To finish

… Rinse 2 basil leaves and chop them.

… Remove the garlic clove, thyme, and bay leaf from the pan. Mash the ratatouille with a fork and sprinkle it with the chopped basil. Spoon half of it into a plate and freeze the rest.

Later, around 14 months

… Add 1 piece of red bell pepper, about 2 ounces (50 g). Peel it with a vegetable peeler, remove all the seeds and ribs, and cut it into small dice.

AD—While you're at it, double the quantities and make a supply of ratatouille to freeze. It'll come in useful, and if you just add 1 ounce (30 g) of minced ham or chicken, you'll have a ready meal at hand.
PN—Even if the bell pepper is peeled, it's not exactly the easiest vegetable to digest. Be patient and wait until baby is old enough before you add it to this dish.

Main Dish

Peruvian Purple Potatoes, Whiting, and Apple

AD–Purple Peruvian potatoes pair well with fish. These long-forgotten potatoes are now easy to find, but you'll have to tell your little ones that not all potatoes are purple!
PN–Of course, but if you can't find them, use ordinary potatoes. These mashed potatoes make a nice change from regular mashed vegetables. And little ones will love eating the apple sticks on their own.

Prepare the potatoes

… Wash and peel 5 ounces (150 g) of Peruvian purple potatoes.

… Cut them into small pieces and steam for 15 minutes, until well softened.

Prepare the whiting

… Carefully remove the bones from a 1-ounce (30 g) fillet of whiting.

… Steam for 5 to 6 minutes.

Prepare the apple

… Meanwhile, peel one quarter of a Granny Smith apple and remove the core and seeds.

… Cut the fruit into sticks.

To finish

… Place the potato pieces in a warmed plate.

… Rinse and dry 1 or 2 sprigs of chives. With a pair of scissors, snip them finely and add them to the potatoes.

… With a fork, mash the potatoes with the chives, adding 1 teaspoon (5 g) of butter and 1 or 2 tablespoons (15 to 30 ml) milk.

… Spoon the mashed potatoes into a plate. Flake the whiting and top the mashed potatoes with it. Stand the apple sticks in the purée.

Eggplant, Tomato, and Mozzarella

Prepare the eggplant and the tomato

… Take an eggplant and cut a piece weighing about 3½ ounces (100 g). Wash it and peel with a vegetable peeler. Cut it into small dice.

… Wash half a beefsteak tomato. Peel it with a vegetable peeler, cut it in two, and remove the seeds. Cut the flesh into small dice and set aside half in a small plate.

… Steam the remaining diced tomato and the eggplant for 5 to 7 minutes, until well softened.

Prepare the mozzarella and pine nuts

… Cut ⅓ ounce (10 g) of mozzarella and dice it. Set aside.

… Heat a small pan and place 1 teaspoon of pine nuts in it. Roast them lightly, until just colored. Drain them on a piece of paper towel and chop them finely. Set aside on a small plate.

To finish

… Rinse, dry, and chop 1 leaf of basil.

… Return the pan to the heat, turn up to high, and pour in 1 teaspoon of olive oil. Place the steamed vegetables in the pan and sauté them with the basil.

… Remove the pan from the heat. Add the diced mozzarella and the diced raw tomato.

… Spoon it into a plate. Sprinkle with the chopped pine nuts and serve.

AD–If your baby is now used to eggplant, you don't need to peel it, otherwise just half-peel it. If she still isn't too enthusiastic about it, remove all the skin because that's what has the strongest taste in this vegetable. PN–Chop the pine nuts really well! Otherwise Baby may spit them out. If you don't have any on hand, substitute a few pinches of ground almonds or hazelnuts.

Main Dish

Carrot, Ginger, and Sesame

AD–This dish of spicy carrots goes with everything: meat, poultry, and fish. You can make it for the whole family and blend just what you need for the little one.

PN–Yes, but if he's already used to eating pieces, there's no need to blend. There are lots of good fatty acids in the sesame. When the ginger is cooked, it's milder in taste. It also contains a good dose of antioxidants.

Prepare the carrots and ginger

… Peel and wash 5 ounces (150 g) fresh bunched carrots, about 3 carrots. With a vegetable peeler, make 2 or 3 shavings and place them in ice water.

… Cut the remaining carrots into fine angled slices.

… Peel 1 small piece (about ½ inch or 1 cm) of fresh ginger. Chop it very finely— you should have about 1 teaspoon.

… Steam the carrots and ginger together for 15 minutes.

… Set aside half in a small plate and keep warm.

… Blend the rest, adding a little formula until the purée is smooth.

Prepare the sesame seeds

… While the carrots are cooking, heat a small pan. Place 1 teaspoon of sesame seeds in the pan and roast until they are lightly colored.

… Drain them on a piece of paper towel.

… Stir them into the blended carrots and ginger, adding 1 teaspoon of olive oil.

To finish

… Rinse and dry 1 sprig of flat-leaf parsley. Pick off the leaves and chop them.

… Spoon the carrot and ginger purée into a plate. Arrange the carrot slices around the plate. Drain the carrot shavings well and insert them into the purée. Sprinkle with chopped parsley and serve.

Cannellini Beans, Croaker Fish, and Balsamic Vinegar

AD—First have Baby taste a piece of plain croaker fish to get used to the taste, and then give him another with a drop of balsamic vinegar.

PN—You can prepare the beans for the whole family. If your fishmonger doesn't have croaker, replace it with another sustainably fished variety, such as porgy, mullet, or whiting.

Prepare the cannellini purée

… A day ahead, soak ⅔ ounce (20 g) dried cannellini or borlotti beans in water.

… The next day, drain them and place them in a saucepan with 1 small sprig of thyme.

… Peel and wash one quarter of an onion and half of a small carrot. Cut them into pieces and add them to the saucepan.

… Cover completely with water and cook for about 45 minutes, until the beans are very soft.

… Remove the pieces of carrot and keep them warm in a small bowl. Discard the thyme.

… Drain the beans and onion, keeping a little of the cooking water, then blend them, adding some of the water to make a smooth purée.

… Season the purée lightly with salt and keep it warm.

Prepare the croaker fish

… Steam 1 ounce (30 g) of skinned croaker fillet for 4 minutes.

To finish

… Rinse and dry 1 or 2 sprigs of chervil. Pick off the leaves and chop them.

… Add them to the bowl of carrots. Pour in 1 teaspoon of olive oil and mix together.

… Spoon the bean purée onto a plate. Arrange the carrots and chopped chervil around the purée.

… Cut the fish into small bite-sized pieces and place on top of the bean purée. Drizzle with a few drops of balsamic vinegar and serve.

Main Dish

Spinach, Watercress, and Goat's Milk Cheese Flan

Prepare the spinach and watercress
… Carefully wash 2 ounces (50 g) of spinach leaves. Remove the stalks.
… Pick off the leaves of 2 ounces (50 g) of watercress and wash them.
… With a knife, roughly chop all the leaves.
… Steam them for just 3 minutes.

Prepare the flan
… In a mixing bowl, break 1 small egg. Gradually add ⅓ cup (80 ml) of formula, beating constantly.
… Beat in 1 teaspoon of whipping cream or heavy cream.
… Season with 1 small pinch of salt and 1 small pinch of freshly ground nutmeg.
… Take the steamed spinach and watercress from the steaming basket and mix into the egg and milk mixture.
… Blend briefly: the mixture should be slightly lumpy.

To finish and bake
… Preheat the oven to 350°F (180°C).
… Pour the flan batter into a small nonstick mold.
… Cut ⅓ ounce (10 g) of goat's milk cheese into small pieces and scatter them over the top.
… Bake for 15 minutes.
… Let the flan cool to lukewarm before serving.

AD–Actually, this is a family recipe (if you adjust the quantities, of course) and a good way of getting everyone to eat spinach!
PN–Spinach is good, full of iron, vitamins, and antioxidants. Watercress is even better. Everyone says that kids don't like both these vegetables, but that's not true!

Zucchini, Shrimp, and Grapes

Prepare the zucchini

… Wash one quarter of a zucchini and one quarter of a summer squash.

… Grate them as finely as possible and place in a bowl.

… Rinse and dry 3 sprigs of chives. Cut them finely with a pair of scissors and mix into the vegetables.

… Wash 1 unwaxed lemon and cut it in half.

… Pour 1 teaspoon of olive oil into the bowl with the vegetables, drizzle with a few drops of lemon juice, and season very, very lightly with salt. Mix together.

Prepare the shrimps and grapes

… Shell 3 pink medium cooked shrimp and cut them into small pieces.

… Mix the pieces into the bowl with the other ingredients.

… Carefully rinse 5 large black or green grapes. With a small knife, cut them in two, remove the skin and all the seeds, and then cut each half into 2 or 3 pieces.

To finish

… Place the grated zucchini and summer squash and the shrimp pieces in a plate or bowl.

… Top with the grape pieces.

… Grate 1 pinch of lemon zest and sprinkle it over the plate.

AD—Make sure you have small, tender zucchini. If you can't find young summer squash at the market, or if they're too large, make this recipe using only zucchini.

PN—If there are any allergies to crustaceans in the family, replace the shrimps with 1 ounce (30 g) of fish fillet or meat, or half a chopped hard-boiled egg.

Crêpes, Belgian Endive, and Ham

AD–Freeze the leftover crêpe batter* and use it some other time to make a batch of crêpes for the rest of the family. This batter is good for both desserts and savory dishes.
PN–Parsley adds vitamins and minerals. The Belgian endive isn't very rich in either, so it's good to add the herb.

Prepare the crêpe batter

… In a mixing bowl, combine 3½ ounces (100 g) of chestnut flour, 2 ounces (50 g) of wheat flour, and 2 pinches of salt. Make a well in the center and break 1 egg into it. Mix well and pour ⅔ cup (150 ml) water and 1 cup plus 1 scant ½ cup (350 ml) part skim/reduced-fat milk, beating constantly.

… When the batter is smooth, cover the bowl with a cloth and let it rise in a warm place for 1 hour.

Prepare the Belgian endive and ham

… Wash 1 half of a Belgian endive. Remove the hard core at the base. Slice the endive into half lengthwise and cut into small pieces.

… Steam the pieces for 5 minutes.

… Rinse and dry 1 sprig of flat-leaf parsley. Pick off the leaves and chop them.

… Blend the pieces of Belgian endive briefly or mash them with a fork.

… Place them in a small saucepan with 1 teaspoon of crème fraîche or heavy cream. Stir over high heat to reduce the cream. Add the chopped parsley and 1 small pinch of fresh nutmeg. Mix together and set aside.

Cook the crêpes

… Melt 1 teaspoon (5 g) of butter in the microwave oven. Brush a small crêpe pan with the melted butter.

… Pour 2 or 3 tablespoons of the crêpe batter into the pan, tilting it so that the pan is evenly covered. Cook until the edges of the crêpe begin to color, then toss it or turn it over with a spatula. Continue cooking for about 1 minute until the other side is done. Make another crêpe using the same method. Transfer them to a plate.

To finish and serve

… Cut ⅔ ounce (20 g) of ham into small pieces.

… Spread the creamed Belgian endives over each crêpe and add the pieces of ham. Roll the crêpes up and serve.

*Batter containing raw egg may be refrigerated or frozen within two hours of mixing. The USDA recommends frozen batter containing raw egg thaw in the refrigerator, not at room temperature.

 Purée

Dried Beans and Chickpeas

AD–In summer, use fresh beans from pods. You'll find white or pink beans at the market—delicious! It takes about 2.2 lbs. (1 kg) to make 4 servings. Add a squeeze of lemon juice and a pinch of paprika to the puréed chickpeas.

PN–Make a quantity of purée suitable for your little one's appetite. The beans, like all other dried legumes, have a high fiber content. Blending them to a purée makes them easy to digest.

Cannellini purée

… A day ahead, soak 5 to 7 ounces (150 to 200 g) of dried cannellini beans in a bowl of cold water. (Allow 2 ounces or 50 g per person.)

… The next day, peel and wash 1 white onion and 1 carrot. Cut them into quarters.

… Drain the beans. Place them in a saucepan and pour in water, making sure they are well covered. Do not add salt. Bring to a boil, skimming several times as the water heats.

… When the water is boiling, add the onion and carrot. Cook over medium heat for 30 minutes. Add 2 sage leaves and 2 to 3 pinches of salt. Cook for a further 15 minutes, until the beans are very soft.

… Take 2 or 3 tablespoons of cooked beans, an onion quarter, and a carrot quarter. Blend them with a little of the cooking liquid and 1 teaspoon olive oil until the purée is smooth.

Borlotti bean purée

… Soak and cook 5 to 7 ounces (150 to 200 g) dried borlotti beans (allow 2 ounces or 50 g per person) as above, adding 1 sprig of thyme, 1 ripe peeled tomato, and 1 red onion, quartered.

… Blend 2 or 3 tablespoons of cooked beans, a piece of tomato, and one onion quarter with a little cooking liquid and 1 teaspoon of olive oil.

Chickpea purée

… Prepare the chickpeas just like the beans, using 5 to 7 ounces (150 to 200 g) dried chickpeas and 1 sprig of rosemary. Blend as above.

Red Lentils, Salmon, and Tarragon

Prepare the red lentils

… Place ⅔ ounce (20 g) of red lentils in a colander. Rinse them well and transfer them to a saucepan.

… Peel and wash 1 small carrot, 2 inches (5 cm) of celery stalk, and one quarter of a scallion.

… Cut the vegetables into large pieces and add them to the saucepan with 1 sprig of thyme.

… Cover well with water. Cook for about 15 minutes, until the lentils are very soft.

Prepare the lentil and vegetable purée

… Drain the lentils, keeping the cooking liquid.

… Retrieve the vegetables, cut them into small pieces, and set them aside in a small bowl, keeping them warm.

… Blend the lentils, adding a little of their cooking liquid until the purée is very smooth. Season very lightly with salt and keep warm.

Prepare the salmon

… Rinse and dry 1 sprig of tarragon. Pick off the leaves, chop 5 of them, and add to the bowl of vegetables.

… Take a 1-ounce (30 g) piece of fillet of organic salmon and check that there are no bones.

… Line the steaming basket with the remaining tarragon leaves and set the salmon fillet over them. Steam for 4 minutes.

To finish

… Mix 1 teaspoon of olive (or canola) oil into the bowl of vegetables.

… Spoon the puréed lentils into a plate and add the tarragon-scented vegetables. Flake the piece of salmon fillet and arrange on the top.

AD–For a variation on this salmon recipe, make it with ⅔ ounce (20 g) of fresh salmon and ⅓ ounce (10 g) of smoked salmon to introduce Baby to the smoked fish.

PN–When he's 2 years old, blend only one quarter of the lentils and combine them with the whole lentils. Before this age, it's best for them all to be blended.

Purée

Corn, Blackberries, and Other Seasonal Fruit

Corn purée

… Remove the husks and silks of 1 ear of corn and wash it carefully.

… Cut it in half. Trim both ends and cut off the kernels.

… In a saucepan, heat 1 teaspoon of olive oil and add the kernels. Cook for 5 minutes over low heat, stirring constantly. Stir in ½ cup (125 ml) of formula, cover with the lid, and cook for 15 to 20 minutes, until the kernels are tender.

… Blend to make a smooth purée.

Corn and mulberry purée

… Rinse 2 ounces (50 g) of ripe blackberries or mulberries and gently pat them dry.

… Place them in a plate and crush them roughly with a fork.

… Arrange them over the corn purée just before serving.

Corn purée with other seasonal fruit

… Depending on what you find at the market, you can replace the blackberries with the same quantity of raspberries, apricots, peaches, or plums.

… If using raspberries, simply crush them with a fork. Cut other fruit into very small pieces.

AD–Use the sweetest corn, available during the summer months, with large kernels, sweeter than those used for popcorn. Corn goes well with fruit: try this recipe with mulberries during their season.

PN–Because corn has a fairly high fiber content, these purées might irritate the still-fragile digestive tract of babies under 18 months, even when blended. Outside corn season, use frozen corn on the cob.

 Soup

Onion, Melba Toast, and Emmental

AD–Baby will have fun pulling on the strings of cheese! It's a good idea to introduce this classic dish of French cuisine bourgeoise early. No need to blend if she's already used to eating pieces.

PN–If you don't have Melba toast or zwieback, simply toast a small slice of bread. And if you double the quantities, you can have a handy meal ready in the freezer.

Prepare the onions

… Peel and wash 2 medium yellow onions (about 10 ounces or 300 g). Slice them and place them in a bowl.

… Season with 1 pinch of salt and 1 pinch of sugar. Stir well.

Cook the onions

… In a nonstick pan, heat 1 teaspoon of olive oil. Add the onions, stir them, and cover with the lid. Cook over medium heat until they are lightly colored and just slightly caramelized, stirring frequently so that they don't burn.

… Pour in 1¼ cups (300 ml) of low-mineral bottled water.

… Stir, lower the heat, and cook for a further 20 minutes.

… Blend the onions only partially so that the soup retains a slightly lumpy texture.

… Pour half into a bowl and keep it warm.

… Let the remaining soup cool and freeze it.

To finish the soup

… In a small plate, crumble 1 slice of Melba toast. Sprinkle the pieces over the onion soup.

… Add 2 teaspoons of grated Emmental or other hard, tasty cheese.

… Stir and serve.

Main Dish

Leek Clafoutis with Aged Comté

Prepare the leek and parsley

… Carefully wash 5 ounces (150 g) of leek whites and slice finely.

… Steam for about 10 minutes, until completely softened.

… Meanwhile, rinse and chop 5 leaves of flat-leaf parsley.

… Place the cooked leek slices in a bowl and stir in the chopped parsley. Place half in a small, heatproof, nonstick tart dish and freeze the rest.

Prepare the clafoutis

… Preheat the oven to 350°F (180°C).

… Break 1 small egg into a bowl. Gradually beat in a scant ½ cup (100 ml) of formula. Beat in 1 teaspoon of heavy cream.

… Season with 1 small pinch of freshly ground nutmeg.

… Sift 2½ level tablespoons (½ ounce or 15 g) of flour into a mixing bowl. Gradually pour in the egg, formula, and cream mixture, beating constantly.

… Pour half of this batter into the tart dish over the leeks.

… Freeze the remaining batter.

Finish and bake

… Grate ⅓ ounce (10 g) aged Comté or other flavorful hard cheese. Sprinkle it over the clafoutis. Bake for 20 minutes.

… Remove from the oven and let cool to lukewarm before serving.

AD–Make your own version of this clafoutis with other sliced vegetables like carrots or parsnips, on their own or combined with leeks or scallions. PN–It's a full meal. Make sure the egg is ultra-fresh—and small, 2 ounces (50 g), or buy pullet eggs. Freeze the leek and clafoutis batter* in a mold, and all you'll have to do for another meal is grate cheese over and pop it in the oven.

---

*Batter containing raw egg may be refrigerated or frozen within two hours of mixing. The USDA recommends frozen batter containing raw egg thaw in the refrigerator, not at room temperature.

Tomato: Variations on a Theme

AD—Actually, this is a recipe for the whole family. When it's the height of tomato season, you should find heirloom tomatoes at the market— they're the best tasting.

PN—The little one won't be lacking in antioxidants, that's for sure, with all these tomatoes. Now's the time to buy a soft skin peeler if you don't already have one. It'll save you from the huge hassle of dipping the tomatoes in boiling water.

Prepare the granita

… Peel and seed 1 medium tomato and cut it into small wedges. Rinse and chop 1 leaf of basil. Blend the tomato and basil together, adding 1 or 2 spoonfuls of water, until the mixture is smooth. Pour it into a freezer bag, seal it, and freeze for 2 to 3 hours, kneading it from time to time so that it forms crystals.

Prepare the chopped tomato

… Peel and seed 1 medium tomato and cut it into small wedges.

… Peel 1 garlic clove, chop one quarter of it, and heat it gently in a small pan with 1 teaspoon of olive oil and 1 small sprig of thyme.

… Add the tomato to the pan with 1 pinch of sugar. Cook over low heat for 10 minutes until all the liquid has evaporated.

… Remove the garlic and thyme. Mash the tomatoes with a fork.

… Let cool.

Prepare the tomato tartare

… Peel and seed 1 small yellow tomato and cut it into small pieces.

… Place them in a bowl. Season with a few drops of olive oil and lemon juice and a small pinch of salt.

To finish

… Place the chopped tomato in a plate and top with the tartar of yellow tomato. Add 1 or 2 scoops of granita and serve immediately.

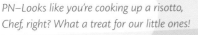

Fields

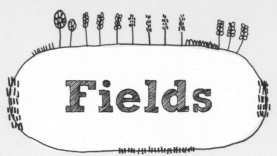

PN—Looks like you're cooking up a risotto, Chef, right? What a treat for our little ones!

AD—It's not just a treat. We're going to introduce them to all the grains: pasta, of course, as well as quinoa and spelt.

PN—Great initiative! Babies need energy: They're growing by leaps and bounds, and grains are the best source of energy.

AD—When they're well cooked, grains can be eaten without chewing. Babies don't have a lot of teeth yet!

PN—Get babies used to chewing early on, otherwise they'll always want soft foods that require no effort. And when they grow up, this contributes to weight gain.

AD—And that's why, here and there, I've included small pieces of cheese, vegetables, fruit, and even truffle! They all go well with grains.

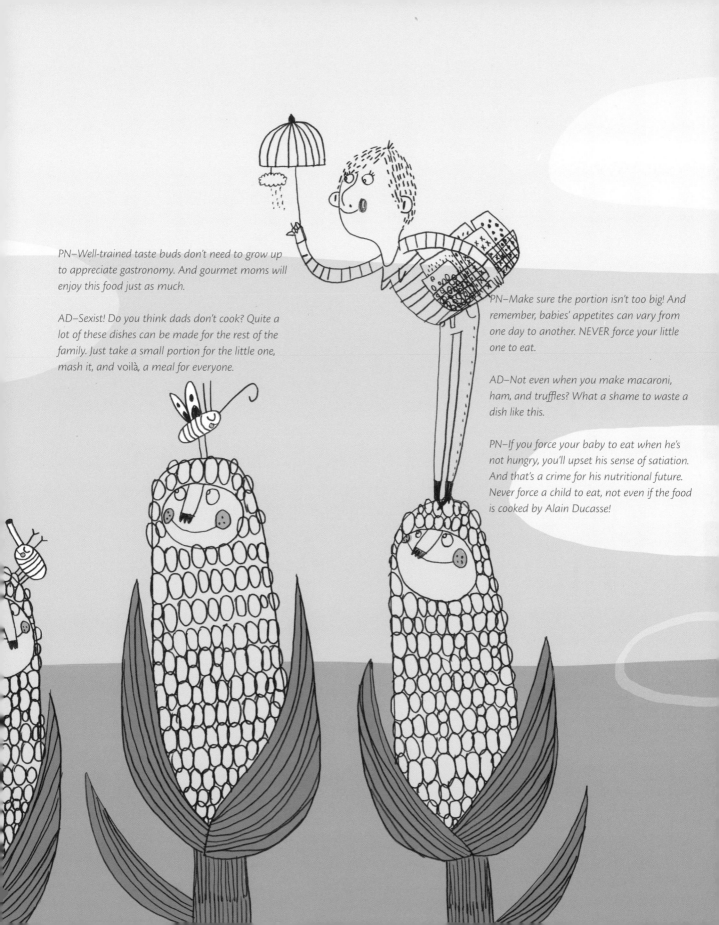

PN–Well-trained taste buds don't need to grow up to appreciate gastronomy. And gourmet moms will enjoy this food just as much.

AD–Sexist! Do you think dads don't cook? Quite a lot of these dishes can be made for the rest of the family. Just take a small portion for the little one, mash it, and voilà, a meal for everyone.

PN–Make sure the portion isn't too big! And remember, babies' appetites can vary from one day to another. NEVER force your little one to eat.

AD–Not even when you make macaroni, ham, and truffles? What a shame to waste a dish like this.

PN–If you force your baby to eat when he's not hungry, you'll upset his sense of satiation. And that's a crime for his nutritional future. Never force a child to eat, not even if the food is cooked by Alain Ducasse!

Bread Sticks, Emmental, and Poppy Seeds

AD–Something tells me Mom and Dad are going to be snatching some of Baby's bread sticks!
PN–They're to help teething. They are so well baked that they're going to be really hard: Baby will suck on them—a lot healthier than an industrially made bread stick full of palm oil!

Prepare the dough

… Dilute ⅛ of a cake of fresh yeast (0.09 ounce or 2.5 g; or 1 slightly heaped ¼ teaspoon of dry yeast) in 3 tablespoons plus 1 teaspoon (50 ml) of lukewarm water.

… Finely grate ½ ounce (15 g) of Emmental or other flavorful hard cheese, preferably aged.

… In a mixing bowl, place 1 level cup (3½ ounces or 100 g) of flour. Make a well in the center and add 1 slightly heaped ½ teaspoon (3 g) of salt, ½ teaspoon (2.5 g) of sugar, 1 tablespoon plus 1 teaspoon (20 ml) of olive oil, the diluted yeast, and the grated cheese.

… Combine the ingredients with your hands, then knead until the dough is smooth and elastic.

… Shape the dough into a ball. Cover the mixing bowl with a damp cloth and let the dough rise at room temperature for 30 minutes.

Prepare the bread sticks

… Cut the dough into 15 small portions. Roll each one on a lightly floured work surface or between your hands to make thin log shapes about 4 inches (10 cm) long.

… In a plate, pour 1 heaping tablespoon of poppy seeds. Roll each log of dough in the seeds. Dust off any excess with a pastry brush. Roll them lightly again in your hands so that the seeds stick to the dough.

… Line a baking sheet with parchment paper. Place the bread sticks on the sheet, ensuring they do not touch.

Bake the bread sticks

… Preheat the oven to 350°F (170°C).

… Bake for 15 to 20 minutes, until golden brown.

… Transfer to a cooling rack or plate and let cool.

Pearl Barley, Pineapple, and Mâche

Purée

AD–Make a bigger amount of puréed mâche and freeze small portions; they'll always come in handy. But be sure to buy mâche (also called lamb's lettuce) that has been freshly picked, not washed and bagged … and washed out.

PN–I totally agree! Mâche has a lot of omega-3, vitamins and trace elements. Make sure the pineapple is nice and ripe, and not out of a can—which is coated with bisphenol A!

Prepare the pearl barley

… Heat some lightly salted water in a pot. When it comes to a boil, throw in ½ to ⅔ ounce (15 to 20 g) of pearl barley. Cook for at least 30 to 40 minutes, until very soft, and drain.

Prepare the mâche purée

… Trim the stalks of 1½ ounces (40 g) of mâche (or lamb's lettuce) and wash the leaves several times.

… Heat some lightly salted water in a pot and prepare a bowl filled with cold water and ice cubes.

… Place the mâche in the boiling water for 2 minutes, drain (keep a little of the cooking liquid), and transfer directly to the ice water so that the leaves retain their color.

… Drain them well and blend with 1 tablespoon of the cooking liquid and a few drops of lemon juice.

Prepare the pineapple

… Cut 1 slice of ripe pineapple weighing about 2½ ounces (75 g). Crush it with a fork or blend it briefly so that it still has pieces.

To finish

… Combine the pearl barley and mâche purée with 1 teaspoon of olive oil and spoon into a plate.

… Top with the crushed pineapple.

Main Dish

9 months

Millet, Vegetables, and Mint

Prepare the raisins

… Place 1 heaping tablespoon of raisins (⅓ ounce or 10 g) in a small bowl. Cover them with water and soak them for 30 minutes until plumped up.

… Drain them and chop them finely with a knife.

Prepare the vegetables

… Peel and wash 1 small new carrot weighing about 1 ounce (25 g) and one half of a small new turnip, about 1 ounce (25 g). Wash a 1-oz (25 g) piece of zucchini. Trim and wash ½ ounce (15 g) of extra-fine French beans.

… Cut all the vegetables into pieces.

… Steam them with a few sprigs of fresh mint for about 10 minutes.

… Blend them with 1 teaspoon of olive oil to make a very smooth purée.

Prepare the millet

… Heat a scant ½ cup (100 ml) of formula in a saucepan. When it comes to a boil, pour in ⅔ ounce (20 g) of millet. When the liquid starts boiling again, turn the heat down, cover with a lid, and cook for about 10 minutes, until soft, and drain.

… Stir in the chopped raisins.

To finish

… Rinse, dry, and finely chop 2 leaves of mint. Stir into the millet.

… Transfer the millet to a plate, pour the vegetable purée over, and serve.

AD–In winter, you can make this recipe with pumpkin or butternut squash (delicious!), mâche, and carrots, of course. Let the seasons guide your choice.

PN–Finely chopped raisins are excellent to get Baby used to small pieces. As they're sweet, she'll enjoy chewing on them and is less likely to spit them out.

10 months

Polenta, Zucchini, and Savory

Prepare the zucchini

… Wash 1 zucchini weighing about 5 ounces (150 g). Trim the tips and cut it in half. Cut one half into very small dice and the other into larger pieces.

… Steam the larger pieces for 10 minutes with 1 small sprig of fresh savory.

… In the meantime, heat a small pan with 1 drop of olive oil. Sauté the small zucchini dice over high heat for 2 minutes, then reduce the heat and cover with a lid. Continue cooking the zucchini until very tender. Remove from the pan and keep warm.

… Remove the sprig of savory from the steaming basket. Pick off 2 or 3 leaves and blend them with the zucchini. Keep the purée warm.

Prepare the polenta

… Heat ⅔ cup (150 ml) of formula in a saucepan. When it comes to a boil, throw in ½ to ⅔ ounce (15 to 20 g) of polenta. Stir briskly and cook for 7 to 8 minutes. Remove the saucepan from the heat and let the polenta rest for 2 to 3 minutes until it swells up.

… Stir in 1 teaspoon (5 g) of butter and 1 teaspoon of grated Parmesan and mix well.

To finish

… Mix the zucchini purée into the polenta.

… Spoon it into a plate, add the small zucchini dice, and serve.

AD–Polenta also goes deliciously with Ratatouille (page 49). Make an extra portion to freeze; it'll always come in handy. This dish takes only 10 minutes to make.

PN–Sure, but ratatouille is for later. If you add ⅔ ounce (20 g) of a fish fillet or chicken, it makes a nourishing meal for the little one. Nice, soft cubes of zucchini are perfect to get Baby used to little pieces.

Main Dish

Risoni, Chicken, and Summer Vegetables

AD–This purée works as a bolognaise sauce! You can revisit it with other vegetable purées, depending on the season. And with fish, meat, veal, beef, or pork.

PN–Risoni are minute! I think they're just perfect for introducing a baby to pasta. If she's still clamoring for purées, mash some of the pasta with a fork.

Prepare the summer vegetable purée

… Prepare or defrost about 3½ ounces (100 g) of Summer Vegetables (page 43).

… Heat it gently.

Prepare the chicken fillet

… Cut a small piece of chicken breast weighing ⅔ ounce (20 g).

… Steam it for 4 to 5 minutes.

… Mince it very finely.

Prepare the risoni

… Bring some very lightly salted water to a boil in a saucepan. Drop ⅔ ounce (20 g) of risoni in and cook for about 4 minutes, until the small pasta is very tender.

… Drain the pasta.

To finish

… Gently heat 1 teaspoon of olive oil in a small saucepan.

… Spoon in the pasta and chopped chicken and mix. Mix in the Summer Vegetables.

… Transfer to a plate and sprinkle with 2 teaspoons of grated Parmesan.

Risotto, Scallion, and Pumpkin

Prepare the risotto

… Cut a piece of scallion just under 1 inch (2 cm) (keep the rest for another recipe). Wash it and cut it into tiny dice.

… Pour a scant ½ cup (100 ml) of vegetable stock into a saucepan and heat.

… In another saucepan, heat ½ teaspoon of olive oil over low heat. Gently soften the diced scallion for 2 to 3 minutes.

… Pour in ½ to ⅔ ounce (15 to 20 g) of Arborio rice and stir well for 2 to 3 minutes, until the rice is well coated with the oil.

… Pour in the vegetable stock, stir, and cook gently, until the rice has absorbed all the liquid. Stir from time to time.

Prepare the pumpkin

… Cut 3½ to 5 ounces (100 to 150 g) of peeled pumpkin, carefully remove any seeds, and cut it into small dice.

… Steam for 8 minutes.

… Blend half of the dice to make a very smooth purée. Set aside the rest.

To finish

… Add the puréed pumpkin to the risotto in the pan. Mix to combine and stir in 1½ teaspoons of grated Parmesan.

… Arrange the pumpkin risotto in a plate. Make a little well on the top, spoon in the diced pumpkin, and serve.

AD–This is another dish that can be cooked for everyone. For adults, add a little butter before the Parmesan. PN–If you don't have homemade vegetable stock, just use water for the risotto, definitely not store-bought cubes full of salt and additives.

Main Dish

Macaroni, Ham, and Truffle

AD–Now's a good time to introduce Baby to this treasure of gastronomy: the truffle! And the entire family will enjoy the dish. Cook 1½ to 2 ounces (40 to 50 g) of pasta per person so you can use a whole jar of truffle pieces. Just less than half an ounce (12 g) is enough.

PN–Or else you can also use a small fresh truffle. Cut it into pieces for the adults and grate a little into Baby's pasta. And it's a good idea to give him a small piece to suck on.

Prepare the macaroni
… Drop ⅔ to 1 ounce (20 to 25 g) of macaroni into lightly salted boiling water.

… Cook until very tender (a little longer than the directions on the packet).

Prepare the ham
… Take a piece of brine-cooked ham weighing ⅔ ounce (20 g), cut into small pieces, and set aside.

Prepare the truffle
… Take 1 teaspoon of truffle pieces from a jar.

… Cut any pieces that seem too large.

To finish
… Drain the pasta and return them to the hot saucepan.

… Add 1 teaspoon (5 g) of butter and stir it in to melt.

… Stir in the pieces of ham and truffle.

… Stir in 1 teaspoon truffle juice from the jar.

… Transfer to a plate and serve.

 Preparation 10 minutes  Cooking 20 to 25 minutes

Einkorn, Fennel, and Sea Bream

AD–Make sure to use einkorn rather than large spelt, which is firmer and not as tasty. If you don't have homemade vegetable stock, simply use water.

PN–Fennel's ultra-rich in vitamins, trace elements, and antioxidants— really good for the little one. But it's also rich in fiber, so wait until he's 1 year old before you give him any, and adapt the quantity to his appetite.

Prepare the einkorn

... A day ahead, soak ⅔ to 1 ounce (20 to 25 g) of einkorn in water.

... The next day, heat 1¼ cups (300 ml) of vegetable stock. Drain the einkorn and throw it into the boiling liquid. Simmer gently for 15 to 20 minutes, until the grains are very soft. Drain and keep warm.

Prepare the fennel

... Cut a piece of fennel weighing 3½ to 4 ounces (100 to 120 g). Wash it and blend it briefly or chop it into small dice.

... Set aside 2 teaspoons of the chopped fennel.

... Heat a saucepan with 1 teaspoon of olive oil. Add the remaining chopped fennel with 1 small sprig of lemon thyme. Cook over low to medium heat, stirring frequently, until very soft.

... Squeeze the juice of ½ an unwaxed orange (reserve the zest). Pour it into the saucepan to deglaze. Discard the sprig of lemon thyme.

Prepare the sea bream

... Place 1 sprig of lemon thyme in a steam basket. Check a ⅔-ounce (20 g) fillet of sea bream for bones and steam it on the lemon thyme for 3 minutes.

To finish

... Spoon the einkorn into the saucepan with the orange-scented fennel and add the leftover raw diced fennel. Stir in 1 pinch of grated orange zest.

... Arrange the einkorn and fennel in a plate and flake the sea bream fillet over. Serve.

Pasta, Broccoli, and Cheddar

Prepare the pasta

… Cook ⅔ to 1 ounce (20 to 25 g) of small pasta in boiling salted water until very soft.

… Drain, shaking the colander to remove all excess water.

Prepare the broccoli

… While the pasta is cooking, cut 15 broccoli florets, removing the stems, and wash them.

… Steam for 5 minutes.

Prepare the gratin

… Preheat the oven to 400°F (200°C).

… Grate ⅔ ounce (20 g) of cheddar.

… In a mixing bowl, mix half of the cheddar with 1½ teaspoons of crème fraîche (or heavy cream) and 2 teaspoons of fromage blanc (or unsalted ricotta or plain yogurt). Give 1 grind of the pepper mill.

… Carefully stir in the broccoli florets.

… Arrange the pasta in a small gratin dish.

… Add the broccoli and cream mixture and stir together.

… Sprinkle with the remaining grated cheddar.

… Bake in the oven for 5 minutes, until nicely browned.

… Let cool a little before serving.

AD–Depending on the season, you can bake this dish with other vegetables: French beans, pumpkin, zucchini, and more. Choose small, fun-shaped pasta, like mini-fusilli or mini-farfalle, either colored or plain. PN–This gratin dish is suitable for everyone, and if there are other children in the family, it's a good way to get them to eat vegetables. Don't add salt to the cream and fromage blanc mixture–the cheddar has enough in it.

Pasta, Turmeric, and Bell Peppers

Prepare the bell peppers

… Wash one ⅓-ounce (10 g) piece of red pepper, one ⅓-ounce (10 g) piece of yellow pepper, and one ⅓-ounce (10 g) piece of green pepper.

… Peel with a vegetable peeler and remove all the seeds, ribs, and any fibers.

… Cut into very small dice.

… Rinse 3 leaves of basil.

… Place the basil leaves in a steaming basket and arrange the diced pepper over them. Steam for 10 minutes.

Prepare the pasta

… Bring some lightly salted water to a boil with a small pinch of ground turmeric.

… Drop in ⅔ to 1 ounce (20 to 25 g) of gnocchetti (or another type of pasta) and cook according to the directions.

… Drain well.

To finish

… In a small saucepan, pour 1 teaspoon of olive oil and heat over medium heat.

… Add the diced pepper, stir, and cook for 2 minutes.

… Add the drained pasta to the saucepan and mix well.

… Transfer to a plate and serve.

AD–Instead of peppers, you can spice up this pasta dish with bottarga, those oh-so-delicious mullet eggs. Cut a small slice, remove the wax, and grate the bottarga into the pasta.
PN–With the olive oil from the bell peppers, there's no need to add butter to the pasta. But if you make the recipe with bottarga, stir in 1 teaspoon (5 g) of butter.

 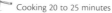

Quinoa, Tomato, and Scorpion Fish

AD–You can also use red quinoa or quinori, a mixture of quinoa, rice, and chickpeas—but only once Baby's tasted white quinoa.

PN–Whether you're cooking white or red quinoa, you should always wash it well to remove all the saponin that coats the grains. It gives a bitter taste and is not easily digestible, but it dissolves in water. If you can't find scorpion fish, use another lean, flaky fish, such as sea bass, red snapper, or grouper.

Prepare the quinoa

… Fill a mixing bowl with water. Pour in ⅔ to 1 ounce (20 to 25 g) of quinoa and rub the grains with your hands. Drain in a colander and rinse under cold running water.

… Bring some lightly salted water to a boil in a saucepan. Throw in the quinoa and cook it for 15 to 20 minutes, until very soft.

Prepare the tomato

… Peel 1 medium beefsteak tomato with a soft skin peeler or by plunging it briefly in boiling water. Cut it into quarters and remove the seeds.

… Cut one of the quarters into small dice and set aside.

… Rinse 1 leaf of basil and snip it with a pair of scissors.

… Blend the remaining tomato with the chopped basil, adding, if necessary, a drop of mineral water.

Prepare the scorpion fish

… Check that there are no bones left in a 1-ounce (30 g) piece of scorpion fish fillet. Steam for 5 minutes.

To finish

… Drain the quinoa and mix it with the blended tomato, the diced raw tomato, and 1 teaspoon of olive oil. Arrange in a plate.

… Flake the scorpion fish fillet over the quinoa and drizzle with a few drops of lemon juice.

Rice, Mushrooms, and Hazelnuts

AD–This recipe works just as well with pasta, quinoa, or millet. But I do like the combination of wild rice and basmati, and Thai rice is good too. PN–And if you add 1 ounce (30 g) of fish, meat, or poultry, you've got a full meal, without any further complications! No shiitakes? Use only button mushrooms.

Prepare the rice

… Place ⅓ ounce (10 g) of wild rice and ½ ounce (15 g) of basmati rice in a colander and rinse well.

… Heat some lightly salted water in a small saucepan. When it comes to a boil, throw in the rice.

… Cook for 20 to 30 minutes, until both the wild rice and the basmati rice are soft.

Prepare the mushrooms

… Cut the stems off 2½ to 3 ounces (70 to 80 g) of button mushrooms and 2½ to 3 ounces (70 to 80 g) of shiitakes. Wash the caps carefully, pat them dry, and cut them into small pieces.

… Peel 1 clove of garlic and cut off one quarter. Remove the green shoot if there is one, and finely chop the quarter.

… Heat a saucepan with 1 teaspoon of olive oil and the chopped garlic. Over high heat, sauté the mushrooms for 2 to 3 minutes. Lower the heat and cover with the lid. Cook for a further 3 to 4 minutes, stirring from time to time.

… Rinse and dry 1 sprig of flat-leaf parsley. Pick off the leaves and chop them.

… Blend half the mushrooms with half the chopped parsley.

… Sprinkle the remaining parsley over the remaining mushrooms.

To finish

… Drain the rice. Combine it with the puréed mushrooms.

… Spread this mixture in a plate. Top with the chopped mushrooms and parsley.

… Sprinkle with 1 teaspoon of ground hazelnuts and serve.

Rice, Whiting, and Seaweed

Prepare the rice

… Bring ⅓ cup (75 ml) of water to a boil with a little salt (omit salt if using nori).

… Pour in ⅔ to 1 ounce (20 to 25 g) of rice.

… Let the water come to a boil again, then lower the heat and simmer gently until the rice has absorbed all the water, about 15 minutes. Stir from time to time.

Prepare the whiting

… Steam a 1-ounce (30 g) piece of whiting fillet for 3 minutes.

… Flake the fish, checking that there are no hidden bones.

To finish

… Stir 1 teaspoon (5 g) of butter into the rice until it melts. Stir in 1 pinch of organic nori seaweed (optional).

… Arrange the rice on a plate.

… Top with the flaked whiting and serve.

AD–What about adding no salt to the rice, and instead flavoring it with a pinch of nori flakes?

PN–Great idea, Chef! This seaweed is a treasure trove of trace elements and can only do a little one good. But the nori you use must be organic, ideally from Brittany.

Main Dish

Tofu and Tomato Tart and Tartlet

Prepare the pastry dough

… Cut 3 tablespoons plus 1 teaspoon (50 g) of butter into small pieces. Sift together 1⅔ cups (7 ounces, 200 g) of all-purpose flour and ⅓ cup (1¾ ounces, 50 g) of potato starch or cornstarch onto the work surface or into a mixing bowl. Add 2 pinches of salt. Stir well to combine and make a small well in the center. Place the diced butter in the well and, with your fingertips, work the butter into the flour mixture to form a crumbly mixture.

… Add 1 egg and 3 tablespoons plus 1 teaspoon (50 ml) of water and knead until the dough is smooth. As soon as it holds together, stop kneading and shape it into a ball; do not overwork. Flatten the dough, cover with plastic wrap, and chill for 30 minutes.

AD–It's much more fun when everyone has an individual tart. You can garnish them with a little Pistou (page 23) once they've cooled. PN–You can also make individual tartlets for each member of the family. Or use large tomatoes— although little tomatoes are easier for little ones to eat.

Prepare the tomatoes and the tofu

… While the dough is resting, wash 8 ounces (250 g) of red cherry tomatoes and 8 ounces (250 g) of small yellow pear tomatoes. Cut away the stem end.

Prepare the tart and the tartlet

… Preheat the oven to 350°F (180°C).

… Roll the dough out very thinly, under ⅛ inch (2 to 3 mm) thick, and cut out one 8-inch (20 cm) circle and one 3-inch (8 cm) circle. Transfer them carefully to a baking sheet lined with parchment paper. Prick the dough with the tines of a fork and bake for 10 minutes.

… In the meantime, chop 10 black olives and mash 3½ ounces (100 g) of silken tofu. Mix them together with 2 tablespoons of olive oil and 1 grinding of the pepper mill.

To finish

… Remove the tart bases from the oven. Spread the mixture over each base; halve the small tomatoes or slice the large tomatoes, if using. Arrange them in circles, alternating the yellow and red and ensuring they are close together.

… Return to the oven and bake for 30 minutes. Serve the tarts still warm or at room temperature.

PN–Wow, you've really gone all out with fish recipes for our kids, Chef!

AD–Fish, shellfish, crustaceans—it's endless! The variety activates my neurons, just like vegetables do.

PN–Well, I certainly won't complain.

AD–Of course not. You're always going on about how healthy fish is because of the omega-3 it contains. We get the point!

PN–Yes, but there are lots of kids who don't like it, or who are scared of bones.

AD–That's another reason to get them to like it early on. I'm talking about fish, of course, not bones.

PN–And then there are the parents who don't like the smell of fish when it cooks.

AD–When fish is fresh, it smells good. And bones can easily be removed, especially from a small fillet.

Sea

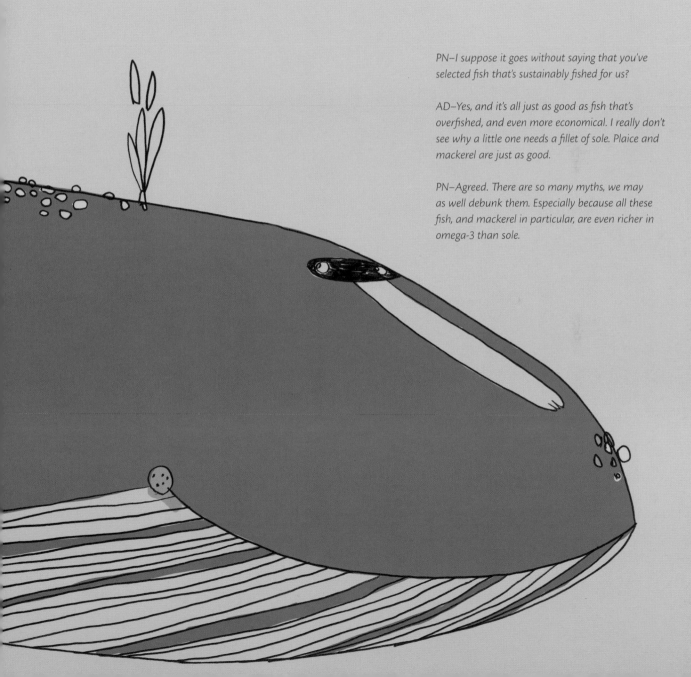

PN–I suppose it goes without saying that you've selected fish that's sustainably fished for us?

AD–Yes, and it's all just as good as fish that's overfished, and even more economical. I really don't see why a little one needs a fillet of sole. Plaice and mackerel are just as good.

PN–Agreed. There are so many myths, we may as well debunk them. Especially because all these fish, and mackerel in particular, are even richer in omega-3 than sole.

Main Dish

Black Cod and Sweet Potato

AD–Later, you can revisit this purée with other, tastier fish, like mackerel. Black cod, which has very little taste, is excellent as an introduction to fish. PN–You can replace the teaspoon of olive oil with the same quantity of canola oil, which is very rich in omega-3 and good for Baby's neurons.

Prepare the sweet potato and black cod

… Peel and wash a piece of sweet potato weighing 3½ ounces (100 g). Cut it into pieces.

… Remove any bones from a fillet of black cod weighing ⅔ ounce (20 g).

… Steam the sweet potato for 15 minutes. Place the fillet of black cod over the pieces of sweet potato and steam for a further 6 minutes.

Prepare the sweet potato purée

… Remove the fish from the steaming basket and keep it warm.

… Blend the sweet potato, gradually adding enough formula and 1 teaspoon of olive oil to make a smooth purée.

To finish

… Rinse 3 leaves of flat-leaf parsley. Chop them very finely.

… Stir them into the purée.

… Flake the fillet of black cod.

… Spoon the sweet potato purée into a plate. Top with the flaked fish and serve.

Plaice, Purple Peruvian Potatoes, and Salted Butter

Prepare the purple Peruvian potatoes

… Peel and wash 5 ounces (150 g) of purple Peruvian potatoes. Cut them into pieces.

… Steam for 15 minutes.

Prepare the plaice

… Remove the skin, if there is any, from a 1-ounce (30 g) piece of plaice fillet.

… Place 1/10 ounce (3 g) of mixed lyophilized seaweed in a bowl of water to rehydrate, then place the flakes in the steaming basket.

… Set the plaice fillet over the seaweed and steam for 3 to 4 minutes.

To finish

… Take 1 teaspoon of cooked seaweed.

… Mash the purple Peruvian potatoes with 1 teaspoon (5 g) of salted butter and the seaweed.

… Spoon onto a plate.

… Cut the plaice into small pieces and scatter them over the potatoes.

AD–If purple Peruvian potatoes are unavailable, make this dish with any heirloom fingerling potatoes in season. It may not look quite as stunning, but it will be just as good.
PN–It's a great suggestion to add seaweed to the purée. I'm all for the idea—it means more trace elements. But no salt, because there's enough in the seaweed.

Main Dish

AD–It's a good idea to use an apple as a vegetable. If you can't find halibut, use a fillet of mackerel or whiting, but be careful to remove all of the bones.

PN–If Baby wants to play with the food in the plate and starts trying to eat alone, she'll like the apple sticks. Otherwise, just cut the apple into small pieces and give them to her with a spoon.

Halibut, Apple, and Curry

Prepare the apple

… Peel 1 Golden Delicious apple weighing 5 to 7 ounces (150 to 200 g). Cut it into quarters and remove the core. Cut three of the quarters into pieces and reserve the fourth.

… Place the apple pieces in a small saucepan with 1 teaspoon of lemon juice, 1 teaspoon of agave syrup, 1 teaspoon of olive oil, and 1 tablespoon of fromage blanc (or unsalted ricotta or plain yogurt).

… Mix together and cook for 2 to 3 minutes over low to medium heat.

… Stir in 1 small pinch of curry powder and cook for 1 minute more. Blend the mixture.

Prepare the halibut

… Check that there are no bones in a 1-ounce (30 g) piece of halibut fillet.

… Steam it for 3 minutes.

To finish

… Cut the remaining apple quarter into thin sticks.

… Place the curried apple purée in a plate.

… Flake the halibut and mix it into the purée.

… Insert the raw apple sticks into the purée and serve.

Main Dish

Hake, Grapefruit, and Garden Peas

Prepare the garden pea purée

… Prepare or defrost 3½ to 4 ounces (100 to 120 g) pea purée (page 18).

… Heat or keep warm.

Prepare the stewed grapefruit

… Peel half a grapefruit, removing all the white pith. Detach the segments between the membranes, and carefully remove any remaining membrane.

… In a small saucepan, gently heat 1 teaspoon of olive oil.

… Place half or three-quarters of the grapefruit segments, depending on your baby's appetite, into the saucepan. Cook them very gently, stirring frequently, until they reach a marmalade texture.

… Mash them with a fork and let all the juice evaporate. Remove from the heat.

Prepare the hake

… Carefully remove all the bones from a ⅔-ounce (20 g) fillet of hake.

… Steam for 5 minutes and flake.

To finish

… Spoon the garden pea purée onto a plate. Make a small hollow at the top and spoon in the stewed grapefruit. Sprinkle with flaked hake.

AD–In winter, make this dish with carrot or pumpkin purée (page 10). These vegetables have the same sweetness as the garden peas and will balance the sourness of the grapefruit. PN–If your baby doesn't take to this acidity, counter it with a few drops of agave syrup in the stewed grapefruit. But don't sweeten it too much! You should get him used to sour foods.

Main Dish

Red Mullet, Fennel, and Orange

AD–Fennel will go just as well with another fish, depending on what good buys you find at the fishmonger. You can play around with this recipe as much as you like!

PN–Naturally, you'll be using an unwaxed orange, and it has to be well washed. Freeze any extra purée—it'll come in handy another time. Over the months, as Baby's appetite grows, increase the quantities.

Prepare the fennel

… Wash half a fennel bulb (about 5 ounces or 150 g) and peel and wash 1 small potato weighing 2 ounces (50 g). Cut both into small pieces.

… Wash 1 unwaxed orange. With a vegetable peeler, cut 1 long piece of zest. Squeeze the juice of half the orange and set it aside in a glass.

… Steam the two vegetables with the orange zest for 15 to 20 minutes, until very soft.

Prepare the red mullet

… While the vegetables are steaming, carefully remove all the bones from a ⅔-ounce (20 g) fillet of red mullet. Check that there are no scales remaining on the skin.

… In a small nonstick pan, heat 1 drop of olive oil over medium heat. Place the red mullet, skin side down, in the pan and cook for 2 minutes.

… Turn it over and cook for 1 minute more.

To finish

… Remove the red mullet from the saucepan and place it on a small plate. Cut it into very small pieces.

… Remove the piece of orange zest from the steam basket and discard it.

… Blend the fennel and potato with the orange juice until you have a nice, smooth purée.

… Spoon the purée onto a plate, scatter with the pieces of red mullet, and serve.

Pollack, Leek, and Nutmeg

AD–In spring or summer you'll find small, new leeks. When you do, include a little of the soft green part– your softened leeks will be even tastier. Add a scallion; it's also delicious. PN–And if Baby is still resisting pieces, blend all of the leek with the potato so that he'll be happier to eat the pieces of fish.

Prepare the vegetables

… Make several incisions lengthwise in one leek white weighing 3½ ounces (100 g). Dip it into a large bowl of water and shake it around to remove any earth.

… Drain it and cut it into very fine slices.

… Peel and wash 1 small potato weighing 2 ounces (50 g). Cut it into pieces.

Cook the vegetables and pollack

… Steam the leek slices and potato pieces for 10 minutes.

… In the meantime, remove any bones in a piece of pollack fillet weighing ⅔ ounce (20 g). Place the fillet over the vegetables and steam for a further 5 minutes.

To finish

… Remove the pollack from the steaming basket and flake it into a small plate.

… Set aside 2 teaspoons of steamed leek slices.

… Blend the remaining leek pieces with the potato, gradually adding a little formula and 1 teaspoon (5 g) of butter. Season with a little freshly ground nutmeg.

… Stir the sliced leek into the puréed vegetables. Spoon into a plate and scatter with the flaked fish.

Main Dish

Lemon Sole, Almonds, and Broccoli

Prepare the broccoli purée

… Take 1 head of broccoli and pick off about 20 florets so that you have about 3½ ounces (100 g). Wash well.

… Peel 1 small potato weighing 2 ounces (50 g). Wash it and cut it into pieces.

… Steam the potato with the broccoli for 5 minutes.

… Prepare a bowl of cold water and ice cubes.

… Take 4 to 5 broccoli florets and refresh them immediately in the ice water.

… Continue cooking the remaining vegetables for 10 to 12 minutes further.

… In the meantime, wash and dry 1 small sprig of flat-leaf parsley and pick off the leaves. Chop them and set aside in a small plate.

… Blend the remaining broccoli and potato, gradually adding a little formula and then the chopped parsley, until you have a nice, smooth purée. Season it very lightly with salt. Keep warm.

Prepare the lemon sole

… Spread 1 tablespoon of ground almonds in a plate.

… Coat one side of a piece of lemon sole weighing 1 ounce (30 g) with the ground almonds, pressing it down until the almonds stick. Shake it a little to remove any excess. (Coat one side only.)

… Heat a small pan over medium heat with 1 drop of olive oil. Place the lemon sole fillet, almond side down, in the pan and cook for 2 minutes. Turn it over and cook the other side for 2 minutes.

To finish

… Cut the reserved broccoli florets into two or three pieces lengthwise.

… Spoon the broccoli purée into a plate. Cut the lemon sole fillet into small pieces and place them over the purée. Add the cut broccoli florets to the purée and serve.

AD–Ground almonds quickly go rancid, so don't use any from a packet that's been at the back of your kitchen cupboard for ages!
PN–If you wish, you can add just one teaspoon of butter (4 to 5 g) to the broccoli purée, depending on what your baby's eaten at the other meals. She's sure to love eating the broccoli florets with her fingers.

Salmon, Couscous, and Spinach

Prepare the spinach purée

… Prepare or defrost 5 ounces (150 g) of spinach, potato, and parsley purée (page 15).

Prepare the salmon

… Remove all the bones from a 1-ounce (30 g) organic or wild salmon fillet. Season very lightly with salt.

… Spread ½ ounce (15 g) of fine couscous over a plate. Place the salmon fillet over it and press in lightly with your fingers to coat one side well with couscous. Shake it gently to remove any excess. (Coat one side only.)

… Heat a small pan over medium heat with 1 teaspoon of olive oil. Place the salmon fillet, coated side downwards, in the pan and cook for 1 to 2 minutes, just until the couscous turns a light golden color.

… Turn the fillet over and cook the other side for 2 to 3 minutes. Remove it from the pan and discard the oil.

To finish

… Stir 1 teaspoon of crème fraîche or heavy cream into the spinach purée.

… Transfer it to a plate.

… Cut the salmon into small pieces, spread them over the spinach purée, and serve.

AD–Even if the salmon fillet is small, it must be as thick as possible. Otherwise, it will be overcooked, and overcooking destroys the flavor of this fish. Wild salmon is the best choice, if you can find it.

PN–Feel free to add even more chopped parsley to the spinach purée–an extra vitamin boost for Baby.

Prawns, Radishes, and Orange

AD–The prawns must be ultra-fresh! No blood oranges at the market? No problem, just use an ordinary orange. It will be just as good. And you can leave the prawns whole; Baby will have fun using his fingers to eat them all on his own.

PN–It's wisest to wait until Baby is 18 months old to give him crustaceans. But if there's a family history of allergies to these creatures, just replace the prawns with 1 ounce (30 g) of fish.

Prepare the radishes

… Peel 8 pink radishes, wash them well, and grate them finely. Reserve in a bowl.

Prepare the orange

… Wash 1 unwaxed orange. With a vegetable peeler, peel 3 to 4 thin pieces of zest, making sure not to include any white pith. Set aside.

… Peel the orange, removing all the pith, and cut out the segments from between the membranes. Catch all the juice as you work. Cut the segments into small dice and add to the bowl of grated radish.

… Squeeze the orange using your hand to extract the remaining juice. Stir it in to the bowl of radish.

Prepare the prawns

… Cut off the heads of 2 large raw prawns; shell and devein them.

… Place the orange zest in the steaming basket and place the prawns over it. Steam for 4 minutes.

To finish

… Cut the prawns into small pieces.

… Rinse 1 chive sprig. Snip it finely with a pair of scissors, working over the bowl of radish and orange. Stir in 1 teaspoon of olive or canola oil and a small pinch of freshly ground pepper.

… Arrange the orange-scented radish salad on a plate, scatter the prawn pieces over, and serve.

Squid, Cucumber, and Lime Muffins

Prepare the squid and cucumber

… Rinse 2 ounces (50 g) of squid (white part only) and cut it into small dice.

… Peel a 2-ounce (50 g) piece of cucumber. Remove the seeds and cut it into small dice. Set aside.

Prepare the muffins

… Sift ⅔ cup (3 ounces, 80 g) of all-purpose flour into a mixing bowl. Stir in 3 pinches of salt and ¾ teaspoon (3 g) of baking powder.

… Cut 2 tablespoons plus 2 teaspoons (40 g) of butter into small pieces and melt them in the microwave oven.

… In another bowl, break 1 egg and beat it. Add 3½ ounces (100 g) fromage blanc (or unsalted ricotta or plain yogurt), the diced squid and cucumber, and the melted butter. Stir until incorporated. Fold this mixture into the flour.

… Grate the zest of half an unwaxed lime into the batter and stir it in.

Bake the muffins

… Preheat the oven to 350°F (180°C).

… Divide the batter equally between 6 lined muffin pans, filling them to three-quarters.

… Bake for 15 to 20 minutes, until nicely risen and a cake tester comes out dry.

… Transfer to a cooling rack and let cool before turning them out of the pans.

AD—You can make these muffins with shrimp and substitute fennel for the cucumber.

PN—These muffins are really pretty, Chef! The whole family can enjoy them. And little ones will love being able to eat them all by themselves.

Mackerel, Mango, and Dill

AD–First have Baby taste the mackerel rillettes. If this is the first time he's tasting the fish, the fromage blanc softens the flavor and is a welcome addition. Then have him taste the mango, and then the two combined.

PN–Just like sardine rillettes (page 114), mackerel rillettes can be used in other dishes. But don't use canned mackerel, for the same reason: bisphenol A.

Prepare the mackerel rillettes

… Carefully remove the bones from 1 mackerel fillet weighing 1½ ounces (40 g).

… Steam for 5 minutes.

… Remove the skin and cut the flesh into small pieces. Mash with a knife, incorporating 2 teaspoons of fromage blanc (or unsalted ricotta or plain yogurt). Season very lightly with salt.

Prepare the mango and dill

… Cut 1 piece of mango weighing 3½ ounces (100 g), remove the skin, and cut it into small dice.

… Place the diced mango in a small bowl.

… Rinse, dry, and chop 2 dill fronds. Add them to the diced mango and season with a squeeze of lemon juice and a little freshly ground pepper. Mix well.

To finish

… Spread the mackerel rillettes in a plate.

… Top with the dill-scented mango and serve.

Scallop, Citrus, and Hokkaido Squash

Prepare the Hokkaido squash purée

… Peel 1 piece of Hokkaido squash weighing about 8 ounces (250 g). Carefully remove all fibers and cut the flesh into pieces.

… Steam the squash for about 25 minutes, until it is very soft.

… Set aside 1 or 2 tablespoons of pieces and keep warm.

… Squeeze the juice of 1 unwaxed orange. Reserve the peel.

… Blend the remaining Hokkaido squash with the orange juice, leaving the purée a little lumpy. Alternatively, mash it with a fork, adding the juice. Keep it warm.

Prepare the scallop

… Wash 1 large scallop under running water. Remove all the membrane and coral so that only the white part is left and pat the scallop dry with a paper towel.

… Steam for 3 to 4 minutes, ensuring that it remains soft.

To finish

… Dice the scallop and place the pieces in a bowl.

… Add 1 teaspoon of olive oil. Grate 1 small pinch of orange zest and 1 small pinch of unwaxed lemon zest over the scallop. Add a few drops of lemon juice and mix well.

… Take the whole pieces of Hokkaido squash and stir them into the purée.

… Spoon the purée onto a plate. Top with the diced citrus-scented scallop and serve.

AD–Have your fishmonger open the scallops so that you're sure they're fresh. Don't buy shelled scallops soaking in a white-ish liquid—they may well have preservatives. Hokkaido squash, also known as red kuri, is a sweet, firm winter squash; try butternut, delicata, or kabocha if you can't find it.

PN–This is a great seasonal dish! It's never too early to learn about the seasons, even if Baby doesn't really realize that scallop season is from November to March.

Sardine, Crudités, and Pistou Sandwich

AD–Naturally the sardines must be ultra-fresh. This recipe can only be made during their fishing season, from March to September, depending on where you live. You can also use albacore tuna or mackerel, again, ultra-fresh, of course.

PN–Don't resort to sardines packed in oil. The bisphenol A that inevitably lines canned food should be avoided. It's been removed from baby bottles but not from cans.

Prepare the sardine rillettes

… With a pair of clean tweezers, remove the bones from 2 to 3 fresh sardine fillets weighing 1½ ounces (40 g) altogether.

… Steam for 5 minutes. Mash with a fork, adding 2 teaspoons of fromage blanc (or unsalted ricotta or plain yogurt), 1 squeeze of lemon juice, and a small pinch of freshly ground pepper.

Prepare the vegetables

… Peel and wash 1 small radish, 2 inches (4 to 5 cm) of celery stalk (this should weigh ⅔ ounce or 20 g), 1 piece of carrot weighing 1 ounce (30 g), and 1 piece of cucumber weighing 2 ounces (50 g). Remove the cucumber seeds. Finely grate each of the vegetables and combine in a mixing bowl. Season with 2 teaspoons of Pistou (page 23).

Prepare the sandwich

… Spread the sardine rillettes over 1 slice of sandwich bread and spoon the grated vegetables over.

… Top with 1 more slice of bread, pressing down lightly so that it holds together. Trim off the crusts.

To finish

… Arrange sandwich quarters on a plate and serve.

Crab, Avocado, and Belgian Endive

Prepare the crab

… Shell 1 claw of a cooked crab. Flake the meat between your fingers, taking care not to leave any cartilage. Set aside.

Prepare the Belgian endive

… Wash 1 red endive and 1 white endive. Discard all the large leaves (keep them to use in a soup). Detach some of the small, tender leaves from the interior.

Prepare the avocado

… With a teaspoon, scoop out the flesh of half an avocado. Keep the skin.

… Blend the flesh with 1 squeeze of lemon juice until it is smooth.

… Add 2 teaspoons of fromage blanc (or unsalted ricotta or plain yogurt) and three quarters of the crab flesh. Season very lightly with salt and stir to combine.

To finish

… Spoon the avocado and crab mixture into the avocado skin.

… Make a little hollow and fill it with the remaining crab flesh.

… Insert a few Belgian endive leaves and serve.

AD—A nutcracker is essential here to break the crab claw. You can also cook a live crab in a court bouillon if you come across one at the fishmonger. The whole family can enjoy it.
PN—Be careful of the small shards of shell. Go through the meat very carefully, otherwise Baby won't be happy with you. He'll probably spit it out, but better that than swallowing the shards.

AD–You didn't want me to prepare lots of meat and poultry recipes.

PN–Because it's not difficult to add about 1 ounce (20 to 40 g) of chopped meat to a purée or to a dish of vegetables or grains.

AD–Quite right. There's always a small piece handy in the fridge.

PN–You should only let Baby taste meat and poultry from seven months, no earlier.

AD–It's true that with just ⅓ ounce (10 g), the allowance for that age, you can't really create wonders of culinary art.

PN–After that, it's ⅔ ounce (20 g) until the twelfth month. Increase to 1 ounce (30 g) between 12 and 18 months, and to 1½ ounces (40 g) up to 2 years. Only at age 3 should babies be given 2 ounces (50 g). Otherwise, their protein intake is too high.

AD–But at the speed they grow, they need protein!

PN–There's plenty of protein in milk, which is, after all, the basis of an infant's diet until at least the age of one. And there are all the other dairy products too.

AD–Okay…I'm busy making my herb crust for the veal. It's going to be delicious. It's for an eighteen-month-old, and I weighed 1 ounce (30 g) very carefully!

PN–Just the right portion. Parents always tend to give their children too much meat. It won't make them bigger, stronger, more beautiful, or more intelligent.

AD–Okay, okay…

Parmentier of Duck and Sweet Potato

AD–The duck breast should be on the family menu, of course! Later on, you can add a hint of quatre épices *(a French spice mixture of black pepper, nutmeg, cloves, and cinnamon) or allspice to the mashed sweet potatoes, just to add a little zing and familiarize Baby with spices.*

PN–The day the family is having a roast leg of lamb, cut off a piece weighing ⅔ ounce (20 g), make a little mashed potato, and voilà*, another type of parmentier. Whatever kind you make, be sure to let it cool a little when you take it out of the oven. You wouldn't want Baby to get burned with the cheese.*

Prepare the sweet potato purée
… Peel and wash 1 piece of sweet potato weighing about 4 ounces (125 g). Cut it into pieces.
… Steam for 15 minutes.
… Blend the sweet potato, gradually adding a little formula, to make a very smooth purée.

Prepare the duck breast
… From 1 duck breast cooked until pink, take ⅔ ounce (20 g) of meat and chop it very finely.

To finish
… Set the oven to broil.
… Add 1 small knob of butter (3 to 4 g) to the hot sweet potato purée. Mix it in until completely melted and incorporated.
… In a small ovenproof dish, place half the chopped duck. Cover it with half the mashed sweet potato. Spread the remaining chopped duck over this and finish with a layer of mashed sweet potato. Smooth the top.
… Sprinkle 1 tablespoon of grated Emmental cheese over the top and cook for 5 minutes, just until the cheese has melted.
… Let cool slightly and serve.

Pork, Parsnip, and Pear

Prepare the parsnip purée

... Peel and wash a piece of parsnip weighing 3½ ounces (100 g). Cut it into small pieces.

... Peel half a pear and cut it into two pieces. Remove the seeds and core. Cut three-quarters into pieces and the remaining part (which should fill about 1 teaspoon when cut) into very small dice. Set aside the small dice.

... Steam the pieces of parsnip and larger pieces of pear for 15 minutes, until very tender.

... Blend them, gradually adding a little formula, until you have a very smooth purée.

... Stir in 1 teaspoon of crème fraîche or heavy cream.

Prepare the pork

... Using 1 slice of well-cooked pork roast, cut a piece weighing ⅔ ounce (20 g).

... Chop it very finely.

To finish

... Spoon the parsnip and pear purée onto a plate.

... Top with the chopped roast pork and the finely diced pear and serve.

AD–Now here's a good way to introduce your little one to parsnips. Buy one that's really fresh, because its flavor deteriorates rapidly once exposed to the air. And get a medium-sized parsnip—it will have a smooth skin and be easier to peel.
PN–There's no carotene in parsnips, as their pale color indicates. But that's not an issue, as carrots so often feature on the menu! And parsnips are full of B-group vitamins. If your little one still isn't too keen on pieces, mash the pear with a fork.

Yogurt-Marinated Chicken, Lemon, and Corn

AD–This yogurt marinade tenderizes the chicken breast, which tends to be somewhat dry. Steam the chicken until it is just done; don't overcook it. PN–You might want to add some ripe fruit to the corn purée. In summer you have a wide choice.

Prepare the chicken

… Cut a piece of chicken breast weighing at least 1 ounce (30 to 35 g) into small pieces and transfer them to a plate.

… Squeeze the juice of one quarter of an unwaxed lemon (save the peel) and drizzle it over the chicken.

… Add 2 teaspoons of Greek yogurt and mix well.

… Cover the plate with plastic wrap and place in the refrigerator to marinate for 30 minutes.

Prepare the corn purée

… While the chicken is marinating, prepare or defrost 5 ounces (150 g) of corn purée (page 65).

… Season it very lightly with salt.

Cook the chicken white

… Drain the chicken pieces, discarding the marinade. Steam the chicken for 5 minutes.

To finish

… Spoon the purée onto a plate. Drizzle it with a little more yogurt.

… Spread the chicken pieces over the purée.

… Grate 1 or 2 pinches of lemon zest over the dish and serve.

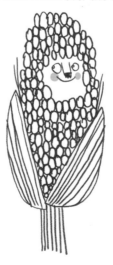

Main Dish

Tagine of Lamb and Dried Apricots with Couscous

Prepare the couscous and dried apricots

… Pour ⅔ to 1 ounce (20 to 25 g) of couscous into a bowl. Bring 1¼ cups (300 ml) of water to a boil and pour it over the couscous. Cover the bowl and let the couscous swell for 15 minutes. Keep warm.

… Cut 3 dried apricots into small dice.

Prepare the tagine

… Peel and wash one quarter of a red onion. Dice it finely.

… Cut 1 ounce (30 g) of leg of lamb into very small bite-size pieces.

… Heat a small pan with 1 teaspoon of olive oil. Place the diced onion in the pan and cook over medium heat for 2 to 3 minutes, until softened.

… Add the pieces of lamb and sear them for 1 minute, turning them until done on all sides.

… Add 2 teaspoons of raisins and the diced apricots to the pan.

… Pour in about ¼ cup (50 ml) of vegetable stock and stir well.

… Add 3 saffron threads and mix well.

… Reduce the heat to low, cover with a lid, and simmer for 15 minutes.

To finish

… Finely chop 1 teaspoon of sliced almonds.

… Remove the pieces of lamb from the pan.

… Blend the diced apricot, raisins, and vegetable stock together.

… Spoon the couscous onto a plate. Make a little hollow and place the puréed apricots and raisins in it. Add the small pieces of lamb, sprinkle with the chopped sliced almonds, and serve.

AD–If you don't have any vegetable stock on hand, simply make this with water.
PN–It would be a good idea to start this meal with finely grated raw vegetables. If your baby's appetite is growing, increase the amount of couscous.

Veal in an Herb Crust with Beaufort

AD–Another take on this recipe is to replace the veal nuggets with small balls of chopped beef or chicken. You'll have enough herbs to make a crust for cutlets for the adults too.

PN–At 18 months, your little one can chew small mouthfuls and she'll enjoy eating on her own. Don't forget to serve vegetables with the nuggets. There's no lack of choice of recipes for seasonal vegetables.

Prepare the herb crust

… Rinse 5 sprigs of flat-leaf parsley and 5 sprigs of chervil. Dry well and pick off the leaves. Rinse and dry 5 sprigs of chives and chop coarsely. Chop the parsley and chervil leaves.

… Process all the herbs with 2½ to 3 tablespoons of breadcrumbs. Spread the herb coating on a plate.

Prepare the veal nuggets

… Flatten a piece of veal cutlet weighing 1 ounce (30 g).

… Make shavings of ⅓ ounce (10 g) of Beaufort or other flavorful, hard cheese such as Emmental or Gruyère, and spread them over the veal. Then fold the piece of veal over itself so that the cheese is in the middle.

… In a soup plate, break 1 quail egg and beat it with 1 small pinch of salt and 1 teaspoon of water.

… In another plate, spread 1 heaping tablespoon of flour.

… Dip the filled veal into the flour and coat it on both sides, then into the beaten quail egg, and finally into the herb coating. Shake very lightly to remove any excess.

… Cut the cutlet into small cubes, just under 1 inch (2 cm), and hold them together with a small wooden skewer.

To cook and finish

… Heat a small pan with 2 teaspoons of olive oil.

… Place the nuggets in the pan and cook for about 5 minutes, turning them over several times.

… Remove the nuggets and place them on a paper towel to drain. Transfer to a plate and serve, removing the skewers.

Pork, Carrots, and Peas

AD–If you find fresh fava beans at the market, you can substitute them for the fresh peas. But be sure to cut up those you set aside, because they're larger than peas.

PN–You might want to finely snip about one inch (2 to 3 cm) of a scallion and sprinkle it over the lettuce chiffonade. If you don't have a leg of pork, use some good-quality sliced ham (not prepared in a factory!).

Prepare the peas

… Shell 7 ounces (200 g) of fresh peas.

… Wash and peel 1 young carrot (about 2 ounces or 50 g). Cut it into fine, angled slices.

… Steam the vegetables together for 15 minutes.

… Set aside the equivalent of 1 heaping tablespoon of the vegetables, reserving the smallest peas.

… Purée the remaining vegetables, gradually adding a little formula, until the purée is smooth. Keep it warm.

Prepare the onion, lettuce, and pork

… While the vegetables are cooking, remove the outer skin of and wash 1 small scallion. Cut the bulb into small dice.

… Wash 1 lettuce leaf and dry it. Remove the large central rib, roll the leaf over on itself, and cut it into a chiffonade.

… Chop 1 ounce (30 g) of cooked pork.

To cook

… Heat a pan with 1 teaspoon of olive oil. Sauté the diced scallion for 2 to 3 minutes, until very soft.

… Add the reserved carrot slices and peas. Mix and season very lightly with salt.

… Lastly, add the chopped pork and stir for 1 minute, just to reheat it.

To finish

… Spoon the pea and carrot purée onto a plate and make a little hollow at the top. Place the contents of the pan in it.

… Spread the chiffonade of raw lettuce over the dish and serve.

Soft-Boiled Egg, Asparagus, and Parmesan

Prepare the asparagus

… Peel and wash 3 green asparagus spears.

… Cut the tips to make spears 2 to 2½ inches (5 to 6 cm) long. (Use the leftover asparagus to make a soup.)

… Steam for 4 minutes.

… In the meantime, prepare a bowl of cold water and ice cubes.

… As soon as the asparagus tips are done, remove them with a slotted spoon and dip them briefly into the ice water. Drain them on a paper towel.

… Let them cool to lukewarm and cut them in two lengthwise. Set aside.

Prepare the soft-boiled egg

… Immerse 1 fresh egg in a bowl of hot tap water for about 5 minutes to bring it to room temperature (if cold out of the refrigerator).

… Transfer it to a steaming basket (or into a pot of boiling water) and cook it for 3 minutes.

Prepare the Parmesan shavings

… With a vegetable peeler, make ⅓ ounce (10 g) of small shavings from a piece of Parmesan. Keep them in a small plate.

To finish

… Place the egg in an egg cup. Cut the top off and insert an asparagus tip into it. Place the other asparagus tips on the plate.

… When Baby has finished eating the yolk and asparagus, scrape the egg white out with a teaspoon and put it on the plate. Add the Parmesan shavings so he can eat them with a teaspoon.

AD—You can also use small sticks of raw vegetables, like carrots of various colors, a celery stalk, and cucumber. Use any remaining vegetables to make a soup.

PN—If you're too impatient to wait until Baby is 2 years old to eat a whole egg, make this recipe with a quail egg. It's the equivalent of half a hen's egg, which is the ration for a 12- to 18-month old.

Orchard

PN–Fruit, fruit, and more fruit, Monsieur Ducasse! It's really good for little ones.

AD–Seasonal fruit from the market, and ORGANIC, of course. Some fruits are accompanied by grains, like small pasta.

PN–Is this a repeat of the spaghetti with strawberries from Nature Desserts? You're right, it's a great combination that provides carbohydrates for energy. Once Baby's eaten this, she'll be raring to go.

AD–Why wouldn't you allow me to use honey to sweeten these desserts?

PN–Because there's a risk of botulism in honey. Bees can carry spores of Clostridium botulinum, which is transformed into toxins in the hive. The risk is minimal (and honey can safely be given from the age of 2 onwards), but we don't want to take it.

AD–You're quite right. I used agave syrup as a sweetener. No risk there?

PN–No, none. Only if you put in too much! And there the risk is that you'll get Baby too accustomed to the taste of sugar.

AD–I used as little as possible. You've been peering over my shoulder constantly, watching what I've been doing, so I couldn't cheat.

PN–Don't complain. If you use too much sugar, you'll also cover the natural taste of the fruit.

AD–Yes, I agree with that.

PN–For once, I've managed to have the last word!

Purée

Apricot, Strawberry, and Blueberry

AD–In winter, replace the blueberries with dried cranberries. Plump them up in water before you blend them or steam them for 10 minutes.

PN–It's advisable to wait until Baby is about 12 months old before introducing any berries, a frequent cause of allergies.

Apricot mousse with pistachios

… Process 2 teaspoons of shelled pistachios to a grainy powder.

… Cut one quarter of a vanilla bean, split it open, and with the tip of a knife, scrape out the seeds.

… Wash 4 ripe apricots, open them, and remove the pits. Cut them into small pieces and blend them with the ground pistachios, the vanilla seeds, and 2 teaspoons of fromage blanc (or unsalted ricotta or plain yogurt).

STARTING FROM 12 MONTHS

Strawberry and banana mousse

… Rinse and hull 2½ ounces (70 g) of ripe strawberries. Peel 1 baby banana.

… Cut the fruit into small pieces and blend them with 2 teaspoons of fromage blanc (or unsalted ricotta or plain yogurt).

Blueberry and pear mousse

… Rinse 2½ ounces (70 g) of blueberries.

… Peel half a juicy pear and cut it into quarters. Remove the seeds and core and cut into small pieces.

… Blend the fruit together with 2 teaspoons of fromage blanc (or unsalted ricotta or plain yogurt).

Purée

Ways with Apple

AD–Forget about the Golden Delicious, which, when all's said and done, doesn't have much taste. Try heirloom apples or ask sellers at your local greenmarket what the sweetest local varieties are.

PN–Don't add any sugar, or any other sweetener, in fact, to the first stewed fruits your baby eats. There's no point in creating an addiction to sugar. The more naturally sweet the apple, the better.

Applesauce with pear

… Peel half an apple and half a pear (both ripe). Cut them into quarters and remove the seeds and core. Then cut into small pieces.

… Steam for 15 minutes.

… When soft, blend the pieces until you have a smooth purée.

Applesauce with prunes or plums

… Soak 2 dried prunes in water to plump them up (this is only necessary if they are not moist). Cut them into pieces, removing the pits. If they are moist, cut them into pieces without soaking, removing the pits. Steam for 10 minutes.

… Blend them with 1 peeled, cut-up apple.

… During the plum season, replace the prunes with 1 or 2 ripe plums.

FROM 9 MONTHS
Applesauce with raisins

… Place 2 teaspoons of raisins in a bowl. Pour in enough water to cover them and leave them to absorb the liquid for 30 minutes, then drain.

… Peel and quarter 1 apple and remove the seeds and core. Cut the quarters into small pieces.

… Steam them for 15 minutes with half the raisins, then blend to make a smooth purée.

… Chop the remaining raisins and stir them into the applesauce.

Purée

Winter and Summer Fruits

Winter fruit compote with walnuts

… Process 2 to 3 walnuts to a powder.

… Peel half an apple and half a pear, both ripe. Cut them into quarters, remove the core, and cut them into small pieces.

… Cut half a slice of pineapple, making sure to remove all the skin, eyes, and core. Cut it into pieces.

… Split open half a vanilla bean.

… Steam all the fruit with the vanilla bean for 10 minutes.

… Remove the vanilla bean. Blend the fruit together, but leave the texture slightly lumpy.

… Transfer the stewed fruit to a bowl and sprinkle with the ground walnuts.

AD–Roast the walnuts in the oven at 350°F (180°C) for 10 minutes before you process them; this improves their flavor. Make enough to have some in reserve so you can use them to dress up other stewed fruit purées.
PN–Remember to give Baby orange juice every day in winter for his vitamin C. Be careful with the nuts—they shouldn't be rancid.

FROM 12 MONTHS
Summer fruit mousse with muesli

… Chop or blend 2 teaspoons of muesli.

… Peel half a ripe peach. Remove the pit and cut the flesh into pieces.

… Rinse 1 ounce (30 g) of strawberries and 1 ounce (30 g) of raspberries. Carefully pat them dry. Hull the strawberries.

… Blend all the fruits with 2 teaspoons of plain yogurt.

… Spoon the mousse into a bowl and sprinkle with the chopped muesli.

Purée

Clove-Scented Pineapple

Prepare the pineapple

… Cut off the skin and remove the core, eyes and any other hard parts of 1 thick slice of pineapple. Cut it into dice.

… Take the equivalent of 2 teaspoons of pineapple and crush it with a fork.

… Wash 1 unwaxed lime and peel 1 small piece of zest.

… Insert 1 clove into one of the pineapple pieces.

… Steam the diced and crushed pineapple with the lime zest for 7 minutes, until very soft.

… Remove the lime zest and clove and blend the diced pineapple (or crush it with a fork) with 1 teaspoon of agave syrup and a few drops of lime juice. (Reserve the peel.) Let cool.

Prepare the pineapple mousse

… In a bowl, pour 1 heaping tablespoon of fromage blanc (or unsalted ricotta or plain yogurt). Beat it with a fork to incorporate some air.

… Add the pineapple purée and beat again.

To finish

… Place the pineapple mousse in a plate. Top it with the crushed pineapple.

… Grate a little lime zest over and serve.

AD–Make sure the pineapple is ripe: You can tell it's ripe if the leaves of the crown can be plucked off easily, but they should not look withered. And the pineapple must smell good, because its fragrance develops over the last days of its ripening period. PN–This is a good way to introduce Baby to pineapple. The mildness of the fromage blanc lessens its sourness, which Baby may not be too happy about.

Anise-Scented Poached Clementine

AD–Instead of the star anise, use half a licorice root—you know, the kind you can chew on.

PN–When clementine season is over, you can also make this dessert with an orange.

Prepare the clementine

... Peel 1 clementine. Separate the segments, carefully removing all white strings.

... Cut each segment into 4 pieces, checking that there are no seeds. Reserve on a small plate.

Prepare the infusion

... In a small saucepan, pour 1 teaspoon of agave syrup and a scant ½ cup (100 ml) of water.

... Add 1 star anise and heat. As soon as the liquid comes to a boil, remove it from the heat.

... Carefully place the clementine pieces in the syrup and infuse for 2 to 3 minutes.

To finish

... Remove the star anise.

... Wait for the dessert to cool. Serve it either lukewarm or cold, but not icy. You may want to crush the small pieces of clementine.

AD–In winter, mashed mango might not be bad. What do you think? And grapes too, peeled and seeded, during their season. You can even use chestnut flakes instead of corn. PN–Mango is super rich in carotenes and antioxidants, so all the more reason to use it. And the same is true of grapes. All good for the little one. You can also use fresh goat or sheep milk if you find any.

Fromage Blanc, Figs, and Cereal

Prepare the cornflakes
… Lightly process 1 heaping tablespoon of cereal or crush with your fingers to make them smaller; the pieces should be very small.

Prepare the figs
… Carefully wash 1 or 2 ripe figs (depending on their size).
… Open them in half and, with a teaspoon, scrape out the flesh.

To finish
… Pour 2 tablespoons of fromage blanc (or unsalted ricotta or plain yogurt) into a plate and spread it out. Spoon the fig flesh over it.
… Scatter with the chopped cereal.

Ways with Yogurt

Apple, pear, and speculoos yogurt

… Blend together a scant ⅓ cup (70 ml) of plain yogurt with 1 heaping tablespoon of applesauce with pear (page 136), 1 teaspoon of agave syrup, and 1 speculoos cookie cut into small pieces. Transfer to a bowl.

… Crumble half a speculoos cookie to fine crumbs. Sprinkle them over the yogurt mixture.

FROM 12 MONTHS
Redcurrant, blueberry, and muesli

… Wash and 2 teaspoons of redcurrants and 2 teaspoons of blueberries. Blend them with ½ cup (125 ml) of plain yogurt and 1 teaspoon of agave syrup.

… Pour the mixture into a glass. Crush 2 teaspoons of muesli and sprinkle it over.

Banana, raspberry and popped rice

… Blend ½ cup (125 ml) of plain yogurt with 1 banana cut into pieces, 2 teaspoons of raspberries, and 1 teaspoon of agave syrup.

… Pour the mixture into a glass and top with 2 teaspoons of lightly crushed popped rice.

Iced yogurts

… Change all these yogurts into frozen treats: Divide the preparation among the compartments of an ice tray. Insert a Popsicle stick into each and freeze for 2 to 3 hours.

AD–These fruit yogurts are better than factory-made yogurts. They're economical, they respect the seasons, and educate Baby's taste buds better. And if you add milk, you have drinking yogurt!

PN–And they're not as sweet. The less sugar you add, the better it is for the little one. Speculoos are crunchy, lightly spiced shortbread biscuits, traditionally made during the holiday season; a gingersnap or shortbread cookie, ideally low-sugar, would also work.

Fall Fruits in Parchment

Prepare the raisins

… In a bowl, place 2 teaspoons of raisins. Cover with warm water and let plump up for 30 minutes.

Prepare the fruit

… Briefly wash 1 fresh fig under running water. Dry it, cut it into quarters, and cut each quarter into two. Place the pieces in a bowl.

… Peel one quarter of an apple and one quarter of a pear. Remove the core and seeds and cut both fruit into small pieces. Add them to the bowl with the figs.

… Split one quarter of a vanilla bean lengthwise and scrape the seeds into the bowl.

Cook the fruit

… Preheat the oven to 400°F (200°C).

… Drain the raisins and mix them into the bowl of fruit.

… Spread a sheet of parchment paper on the work surface. Place the fruits on it and fold over to seal.

… Bake for 7 minutes.

To finish

… Open up the papillote. Grate 1 pinch of unwaxed lemon zest over the fruit.

… Mash with a fork, let cool to lukewarm, and serve.

AD–All these fruits are naturally sweet, so no need to add agave syrup, in my opinion. But when you open up the papillote, you can sprinkle in a little crumble mixture, don't you think? We use it in the Strained Fresh Cheese, Banana, and Cocoa Crumble (page 151).

PN–You're right, Chef. The less sugar you give a baby, the better. I don't have a problem with the crumble but I think it should be served later, at 12 months. And increase the amount of fruit as Baby grows.

Porridge, Nectarine, and Apricot

AD–In winter, you can make this with dried fruit, such as apricots, raisins, and figs. But you must soak them well before. You can also flavor them with 1 teaspoon of orange flower water. PN–Orange flower water has a calming effect. It's natural and not at all toxic, so it's a good idea to use it if Baby is a bit irritable.

Prepare the nectarine and apricot

… Peel half a nectarine, remove the pit, and cut the flesh into small dice. Reserve on a plate.

… Wash 1 small apricot (or half a large one). Remove the pit and cut it into small dice. Reserve with the diced nectarine.

Prepare the porridge

… Pour ⅓ cup (75 ml) of formula into a small saucepan. Heat over medium heat. When it comes to a boil, pour in ½ ounce (15 g) of oatmeal.

… Cook over low heat, stirring constantly, according to directions on the packet.

… Remove the saucepan from the heat and stir in ½ teaspoon (2.5 ml) of agave syrup.

… Mix well and let the oatmeal swell and cool for 10 minutes.

To finish

… Blend (or mash with a fork) three-quarters of the diced nectarine and apricot. Carefully stir into the porridge.

… Spoon the porridge into a plate. Top with the remaining fruit and serve.

AD–This batter makes a clafoutis for four. The fruit must be ripe. Don't think that just because you're going to be cooking it you can select hard, green fruit. Remember that cooking doesn't improve their flavor.

PN–Go easy on the meat or fish for this meal. This dessert, with its eggs and milk, is rich in animal protein, so plan on serving soup or vegetables, some starch, and then the clafoutis as a dessert.

Clafoutis

Prepare the clafoutis batter

… In a mixing bowl, sift ⅓ cup (1½ ounces, 40 g) of flour and combine it with a scant ½ cup (1½ ounces, 40 g) ground blanched almonds and 1 pinch of salt. Add 1 tablespoon plus 1 teaspoon (20 ml) of agave syrup and mix in.

… In another mixing bowl, break 2 eggs and beat them. Pour in 1 cup (250 ml) of reduced-fat milk and beat until smooth.

… Gradually pour the egg and milk mixture into the dry ingredients, beating constantly, until the batter is smooth. There should be no lumps.

… Take 1 ladleful to make the clafoutis and freeze* the rest.

Prepare a cherry clafoutis with almonds

… Preheat the oven to 350°F (180°C).

… Wash 2 ounces (50 g) of cherries, pick the stems off, and remove the pits. Cut them into quarters.

… Chop 2 teaspoons of sliced almonds.

… Butter and flour a small tart mold, 2½ inches (7 cm) in diameter. Turn it over and tap it to remove any excess flour.

… Arrange the cherries in the mold and pour the ladleful of batter over them. Sprinkle with the chopped almonds. Bake for 25 to 30 minutes. It should remain soft inside.

Prepare an apricot clafoutis with pistachios

… Wash 1 large apricot and remove the pit. Cut it into small segments. Chop 2 teaspoons of pistachios. Arrange the apricots in the prepared mold, sprinkle with the chopped pistachios, and proceed as for the cherry clafoutis.

Prepare a plum clafoutis

… Wash 2 ounces (50 g) of plums. Cut them into small pieces and proceed as above, without adding any nuts.

---

*Batter containing raw egg may be refrigerated or frozen within two hours of mixing. The USDA recommends frozen batter containing raw egg thaw in the refrigerator, not at room temperature.

AD–Crêpes go well with all fruits. You can make them with winter or summer fruit compotes, with a slice of pineapple, a peach, or strawberries. PN–And it's also a dessert that's rich in carbohydrates so don't serve too much other starch at the same meal. These crêpes will be good after a dish of vegetables. Adjust the number of crêpes you make depending on how hungry your little one is.

Fruit-Filled Crêpes

Prepare the crêpes

… Make 1 recipe crêpe batter (page 60). Cook two crêpes.

Apricot crêpes

… Wash 1 apricot and remove the pit. Cut it into small dice. On each crêpe, spread 1½ teaspoons of apricot mousse (page 134), arrange the diced apricot over it, and roll up the crêpe.

Apple or pear crêpes

… Cut the equivalent of 1 heaping tablespoon of diced apple or pear. Using the recipe for applesauce with pear (page 136), proceed as above.

Banana and chocolate crêpes

… Peel 1 small banana, cut it into pieces, and mash it with a fork.
… Spread half of it over each crêpe.
… Grate 1 square (5 g) of bittersweet chocolate over the top. Roll up and serve.

Strained Fresh Cheese, Banana, and Cocoa Crumble

Prepare the cocoa crumble

… Preheat the oven to 340°F (170°C).

… Dice 1 tablespoon plus 2 teaspoons (25 g) of butter. Place in a mixing bowl.

… Add 2 tablespoons (1 ounce, 25 g) of sugar, 2½ tablespoons (1 ounce, 25 g) of flour, a generous ¼ cup (1 ounce, 25 g) of ground blanched almonds, and 1½ tablespoons (⅓ ounce, 10 g) of unsweetened cocoa powder. Rub the ingredients together with your fingers until the mixture forms a rough dough with large crumbs.

… Line a baking sheet with parchment paper and spread the crumble mixture out evenly. Bake for about 15 minutes.

… Transfer to a plate and let cool.

Prepare the banana

… Peel 1 baby banana and cut it into thin slices. Place them in a soup plate and squeeze over the juice of one quarter of a lemon so that the banana doesn't blacken.

To finish

… In a bowl, place 3½ ounces (scant ½ cup or 100 g) of strained fresh cheese. Thin it by stirring in 1 spoonful of the liquid that has drained from it, then arrange the banana slices over it.

… Top with 1 or 2 spoonfuls of cocoa crumble.

AD–Keep the leftover crumble preparation in an airtight container. If you can't use it within three or four days, you should freeze it immediately. PN–If your little one is still reluctant to eat pieces, blend or mash the bananas so you're not asking her to eat slices in addition to the crumble. If you can't find faisselle, a strained fromage blanc, you can make your own by wrapping the curds (fromage blanc or unsalted ricotta) in cheesecloth and letting it drain until it has reached a firmer texture.

AD—Anyone who makes this recipe in winter with imported strawberries will have to deal with me! Strawberry season is usually from May to August, with repeat blooming.

PN—Calm down, Chef. Parents know they have to respect the seasons. They also know that because there's a risk of allergy, it's best not to give a baby berries until she's 12 months old.

Strawberries, Alphabet Noodles, and Cranberries

Prepare the noodles

… Bring some lightly salted water to boil in a saucepan. Pour in ½ ounce (15 g) of alphabet noodles and cook them according to the directions on the packet.

… Drain and let cool completely.

Prepare the strawberries and cranberries

… In the meantime, rinse and hull 3½ ounces (100 g) of ripe strawberries. Cut them into small pieces and set aside in a bowl.

… With a large knife, chop 2 teaspoons of dried cranberries and add them to the bowl.

Prepare the strawberry coulis

… Pour a scant ½ cup (100 ml) of cranberry juice (or mineral water) into the bowl of strawberries and cranberries. Add a squeeze of lemon juice and mix. Place in the refrigerator to marinate for 15 minutes, until the cranberry pieces have softened.

To finish

… Pour the mixture into a soup plate and add the alphabet noodles.

… Serve.

Petit-Suisse, Strawberries, Raspberries, and Pink Ladyfingers

Prepare the strawberries and raspberries

… Rinse 2 ounces (50 g) of strawberries in a colander, dry them well, and hull them. Finely dice enough strawberries to fill 2 teaspoons. Set aside the rest to make a coulis.

… Carefully rinse 2 ounces (50 g) of raspberries and carefully pat them dry. Set aside 4 with the diced strawberries.

… Purée the fruit with 1 teaspoon of agave syrup and 2 teaspoons of mineral water to make a coulis texture.

Prepare the pink ladyfingers

… Crush half a pink ladyfinger to fine crumbs. Reserve on a small plate.

To finish

… Remove the paper from one 2-ounce (60 g) petit suisse (or make a scoop of unsalted ricotta) and carefully set it in a plate.

… Pour in the strawberry and raspberry coulis, then arrange the finely diced pieces of strawberry and the whole raspberries over and around it.

… Sprinkle with the crumbed ladyfingers and serve.

AD–No petit-suisse in the refrigerator? Use fromage blanc, unsalted ricotta, or other fresh, creamy cow's milk cheese. No pink ladyfingers (Biscuits roses de Reims)? Finely chop some pistachios or almonds. Also try this recipe without agave syrup so that you can get Baby used to a little sourness.

PN–This is a practical dessert that you can interpret in many ways, with pear or apple and mango coulis in winter, for example. And in summer, with peaches, apricots, and plums. All fruits go well with petit-suisse.

AD–Happy Birthday!
PN–Joyeux anniversaire!

First Birthday Cake

Prepare the cake

… Sift together ½ cup plus 1 tablespoon (2½ ounces, 70 g) of flour, ⅓ cup plus 1 tablespoon (2½ ounces, 70 g) of cornstarch, ¼ cup (1 ounce, 30 g) of unsweetened cocoa powder, **and** 1¼ teaspoons (5 g) of baking powder in a mixing bowl.

… In another mixing bowl, crack 3 eggs. Beat them with a fork. Add ⅓ cup (80 ml) of agave syrup **and** ½ cup (120 ml) of fromage blanc or unsalted ricotta. Beat well. Gradually stir in the dry ingredients until combined.

… Stir 4 tablespoons (60 g) of melted butter into the batter until smooth.

Bake the cake

… Preheat the oven to 350°F (180°C).

… Butter and flour a 7-inch (18 cm) pan and pour in the batter. Rap it lightly so that it is evenly distributed.

… Bake for 20 minutes, until a cake tester comes out dry.

Decorate the cake

… Turn the cake out onto a cooling rack and let cool.

… Pour 3 to 4 tablespoons of colored sprinkles into a plate.

… With a vegetable peeler, make shavings from two 1-ounce squares of bittersweet chocolate **and** one 1-ounce square of milk chocolate.

… Break ½ ounce (15 g) of bittersweet chocolate into pieces and melt it in the microwave oven with 1 tablespoon plus 1 teaspoon (20 ml) of reduced-fat milk.

… With a pastry brush, evenly cover the sides of the cake with some of the melted chocolate and press in the sprinkles.

… With a spatula, evenly spread the remaining chocolate over the top.

… Scatter over the chocolate shavings.

To finish

… Place a candle on the cake. Keep the cake in the refrigerator until serving.

Index

First published in the United States of America in 2014
by Rizzoli International Publications, Inc.
300 Park Avenue South
New York, NY 10010
www.rizzoliusa.com

Nature Bébés, simple, sain et bon © 2012 LEC Alain Ducasse Editions

Originally published in French in 2012
by LEC Alain Ducasse Editions
www.alain-ducasse.com

English translation by Carmella Abramowitz Moreau

2014 2015 2016 / 10 9 8 7 6 5 4 3 2 1

Distributed to the U.S. trade by Random House, New York

Printed in China

ISBN-13: 978-0-7893-2725-3
Library of Congress Control Number: 2013948578

Paule Neyrat

Jérôme Lacressonnière with all his family

DIRECTOR OF PUBLISHING
Emmanuel Jirou-Najou

EDITOR
Alice Gouget

EDITORIAL ASSISTANT
Claire Dupuy

PHOTOGRAPHER
Rina Nurra

STYLIST
Lissa Streeter

ILLUSTRATIONS
Christine Roussy

ARTISTIC DIRECTION / CONCEPT
Pierre Tachon / Soins Graphiques

EXECUTION AND MODEL
Nord Compo

PRESS
Camille Gonnet

Jérôme Lacressonnière would like to thank

Alain Ducasse, for allowing me to produce this book.

Emmanuel Jirou-Najou and his team for placing their confidence in me.

Paule, Rina, and Lissa for their professionalism.

The produce sellers at the Sablons market in Neuilly-sur-Seine.

Sophie, Matilda, and Lucie for the support they provide every day.

Gabrielle and her parents for always making themselves available.

Ariane and Thibault, who opened the doors of their kitchen to me.

My family, my friends, and my friends the chefs Armand and Sylvestre for their good advice.

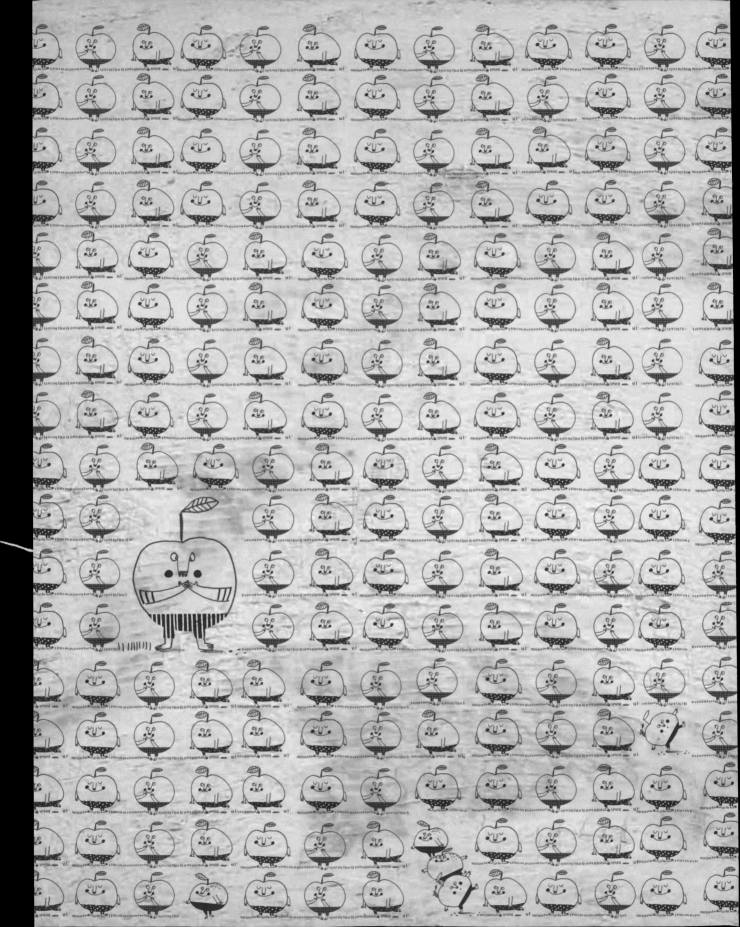